BENITO MUSSOLINI

BENITO MUSSOLINI

Larry Hartenian

CHELSEA HOUSE PUBLISHERS
NEW YORK
PHILADELPHIA

EDITOR-IN-CHIEF: Nancy Toff
EXECUTIVE EDITOR: Remmel T. Nunn
MANAGING EDITOR: Karyn Gullen Browne
COPY CHIEF: Juliann Barbato
PICTURE EDITOR: Adrian G. Allen
ART DIRECTOR: Giannella Garrett
MANUFACTURING MANAGER: Gerald Levine

Staff for MUSSOLINI:

SENIOR EDITOR: John W. Selfridge
ASSOCIATE EDITOR: Jeff Klein
COPY EDITOR: Karen Hammonds
EDITORIAL ASSISTANT: Sean Ginty
ASSOCIATE PICTURE EDITOR: Juliette Dickstein
PICTURE RESEARCHER: Karen Herman
SENIOR DESIGNER: David Murray
ASSISTANT DESIGNER: Jill Goldreyer
PRODUCTION COORDINATOR: Joseph Romano
COVER ILLUSTRATION: Richard Leonard

CREATIVE DIRECTOR: Harold Steinberg

5   7   9   8   6   4

Library of Congress Cataloging in Publication Data

Hartenian, Larry. BENITO MUSSOLINI/LARRY HARTENIAN
p. cm.—(World leaders past & present)
Bibliography: p.
Includes index.
Summary: A biography of the founder of fascism who ruled Italy for
almost twenty-one years, hoping to build a great empire but leaving it a
shambles.
ISBN 0-87754-572-3
    0-7910-0554-2 (pbk.)

1. Mussolini, Benito, 1883–1945—Juvenile literature.
2. Italy—Politics and government—1914–1945—Juvenile
literature. 3. Fascism—Italy—History—20th century—
Juvenile literature. 4. Heads of state—Italy—Biography—
Juvenile literature. [1. Mussolini, Benito, 1883–1945.
2. Heads of state.] I. Title. II. Series.
DG575.M8H33   1988
945.091'.092'4—dc19
[B]
[92]   87-26581
                                          CIP
                                          AC

Contents

"On Leadership," Arthur M. Schlesinger, jr. 7

1. The March on Rome 13
2. Bad Boy Benito 23
3. Young Radical 31
4. "War on Socialism" 43
5. The Fascist State 55
6. Fantasy Empire 67
7. Pact of Steel 75
8. "Appointment with History" 89
9. Mussolini's Last Days 101

Further Reading 108
Chronology 109
Index 110

John Adams
John Quincy Adams
Konrad Adenauer
Alexander the Great
Salvador Allende
Marc Antony
Corazon Aquino
Yasir Arafat
King Arthur
Hafez al-Assad
Kemal Atatürk
Attila
Clement Attlee
Augustus Caesar
Menachem Begin
David Ben-Gurion
Otto von Bismarck
Léon Blum
Simon Bolívar
Cesare Borgia
Willy Brandt
Leonid Brezhnev
Julius Caesar
John Calvin
Jimmy Carter
Fidel Castro
Catherine the Great
Charlemagne
Chiang Kai-Shek
Winston Churchill
Georges Clemenceau
Cleopatra
Constantine the Great
Hernán Cortés
Oliver Cromwell
Georges-Jacques
  Danton
Jefferson Davis
Moshe Dayan
Charles de Gaulle
Eamon De Valera
Eugene Debs
Deng Xiaoping
Benjamin Disraeli
Alexander Dubček
François & Jean-Claude
  Duvalier
Dwight Eisenhower
Eleanor of Aquitaine
Elizabeth I
Faisal
Ferdinand & Isabella
Francisco Franco
Benjamin Franklin

Frederick the Great
Indira Gandhi
Mohandas Gandhi
Giuseppe Garibaldi
Amin & Bashir Gemayel
Genghis Khan
William Gladstone
Mikhail Gorbachev
Ulysses S. Grant
Ernesto "Che" Guevara
Tenzin Gyatso
Alexander Hamilton
Dag Hammarskjöld
Henry VIII
Henry of Navarre
Paul von Hindenburg
Hirohito
Adolf Hitler
Ho Chi Minh
King Hussein
Ivan the Terrible
Andrew Jackson
James I
Wojciech Jaruzelski
Thomas Jefferson
Joan of Arc
Pope John XXIII
Pope John Paul II
Lyndon Johnson
Benito Juárez
John Kennedy
Robert Kennedy
Jomo Kenyatta
Ayatollah Khomeini
Nikita Khrushchev
Kim Il Sung
Martin Luther King, Jr.
Henry Kissinger
Kublai Khan
Lafayette
Robert E. Lee
Vladimir Lenin
Abraham Lincoln
David Lloyd George
Louis XIV
Martin Luther
Judas Maccabeus
James Madison
Nelson & Winnie
  Mandela
Mao Zedong
Ferdinand Marcos
George Marshall

Mary, Queen of Scots
Tomáš Masaryk
Golda Meir
Klemens von Metternich
James Monroe
Hosni Mubarak
Robert Mugabe
Benito Mussolini
Napoléon Bonaparte
Gamal Abdel Nasser
Jawaharlal Nehru
Nero
Nicholas II
Richard Nixon
Kwame Nkrumah
Daniel Ortega
Mohammed Reza Pahlavi
Thomas Paine
Charles Stewart
  Parnell
Pericles
Juan Perón
Peter the Great
Pol Pot
Muammar el-Qaddafi
Ronald Reagan
Cardinal Richelieu
Maximilien Robespierre
Eleanor Roosevelt
Franklin Roosevelt
Theodore Roosevelt
Anwar Sadat
Haile Selassie
Prince Sihanouk
Jan Smuts
Joseph Stalin
Sukarno
Sun Yat-sen
Tamerlane
Mother Teresa
Margaret Thatcher
Josip Broz Tito
Toussaint L'Ouverture
Leon Trotsky
Pierre Trudeau
Harry Truman
Queen Victoria
Lech Walesa
George Washington
Chaim Weizmann
Woodrow Wilson
Xerxes
Emiliano Zapata
Zhou Enlai

CHELSEA HOUSE PUBLISHERS

ON LEADERSHIP

Arthur M. Schlesinger, jr.

LEADERSHIP, it may be said, is really what makes the world go round. Love no doubt smooths the passage; but love is a private transaction between consenting adults. Leadership is a public transaction with history. The idea of leadership affirms the capacity of individuals to move, inspire, and mobilize masses of people so that they act together in pursuit of an end. Sometimes leadership serves good purposes, sometimes bad; but whether the end is benign or evil, great leaders are those men and women who leave their personal stamp on history.

Now, the very concept of leadership implies the proposition that individuals can make a difference. This proposition has never been universally accepted. From classical times to the present day, eminent thinkers have regarded individuals as no more than the agents and pawns of larger forces, whether the gods and goddesses of the ancient world or, in the modern era, race, class, nation, the dialectic, the will of the people, the spirit of the times, history itself. Against such forces, the individual dwindles into insignificance.

So contends the thesis of historical determinism. Tolstoy's great novel *War and Peace* offers a famous statement of the case. Why, Tolstoy asked, did millions of men in the Napoleonic Wars, denying their human feelings and their common sense, move back and forth across Europe slaughtering their fellows? "The war," Tolstoy answered, "was bound to happen simply because it was bound to happen." All prior history predetermined it. As for leaders, they, Tolstoy said, "are but the labels that serve to give a name to an end and, like labels, they have the least possible connection with the event." The greater the leader, "the more conspicuous the inevitability and the predestination of every act he commits." The leader, said Tolstoy, is "the slave of history."

Determinism takes many forms. Marxism is the determinism of class. Nazism the determinism of race. But the idea of men and women as the slaves of history runs athwart the deepest human instincts. Rigid determinism abolishes the idea of human freedom—

the assumption of free choice that underlies every move we make, every word we speak, every thought we think. It abolishes the idea of human responsibility, since it is manifestly unfair to reward or punish people for actions that are by definition beyond their control. No one can live consistently by any deterministic creed. The Marxist states prove this themselves by their extreme susceptibility to the cult of leadership.

More than that, history refutes the idea that individuals make no difference. In December 1931 a British politician crossing Park Avenue in New York City between 76th and 77th Streets around 10:30 P.M. looked in the wrong direction and was knocked down by an automobile—a moment, he later recalled, of a man aghast, a world aglare: "I do not understand why I was not broken like an eggshell or squashed like a gooseberry." Fourteen months later an American politician, sitting in an open car in Miami, Florida, was fired on by an assassin; the man beside him was hit. Those who believe that individuals make no difference to history might well ponder whether the next two decades would have been the same had Mario Constasino's car killed Winston Churchill in 1931 and Giuseppe Zangara's bullet killed Franklin Roosevelt in 1933. Suppose, in addition, that Adolf Hitler had been killed in the street fighting during the Munich *Putsch* of 1923 and that Lenin had died of typhus during World War I. What would the 20th century be like now?

For better or for worse, individuals do make a difference. "The notion that a people can run itself and its affairs anonymously," wrote the philosopher William James, "is now well known to be the silliest of absurdities. Mankind does nothing save through initiatives on the part of inventors, great or small, and imitation by the rest of us—these are the sole factors in human progress. Individuals of genius show the way, and set the patterns, which common people then adopt and follow."

Leadership, James suggests, means leadership in thought as well as in action. In the long run, leaders in thought may well make the greater difference to the world. But, as Woodrow Wilson once said, "Those only are leaders of men, in the general eye, who lead in action. . . . It is at their hands that new thought gets its translation into the crude language of deeds." Leaders in thought often invent in solitude and obscurity, leaving to later generations the tasks of imitation. Leaders in action—the leaders portrayed in this series—have to be effective in their own time.

And they cannot be effective by themselves. They must act in response to the rhythms of their age. Their genius must be adapted, in a phrase of William James's, "to the receptivities of the moment." Leaders are useless without followers. "There goes the mob," said the French politician hearing a clamor in the streets. "I am their leader. I must follow them." Great leaders turn the inchoate emotions of the mob to purposes of their own. They seize on the opportunities of their time, the hopes, fears, frustrations, crises, potentialities. They succeed when events have prepared the way for them, when the community is awaiting to be aroused, when they can provide the clarifying and organizing ideas. Leadership ignites the circuit between the individual and the mass and thereby alters history.

It may alter history for better or for worse. Leaders have been responsible for the most extravagant follies and most monstrous crimes that have beset suffering humanity. They have also been vital in such gains as humanity has made in individual freedom, religious and racial tolerance, social justice, and respect for human rights.

There is no sure way to tell in advance who is going to lead for good and who for evil. But a glance at the gallery of men and women in *World Leaders—Past and Present* suggests some useful tests.

One test is this: Do leaders lead by force or by persuasion? By command or by consent? Through most of history leadership was exercised by the divine right of authority. The duty of followers was to defer and to obey. "Theirs not to reason why / Theirs but to do and die." On occasion, as with the so-called enlightened despots of the 18th century in Europe, absolutist leadership was animated by humane purposes. More often, absolutism nourished the passion for domination, land, gold, and conquest and resulted in tyranny.

The great revolution of modern times has been the revolution of equality. The idea that all people should be equal in their legal condition has undermined the old structure of authority, hierarchy, and deference. The revolution of equality has had two contrary effects on the nature of leadership. For equality, as Alexis de Tocqueville pointed out in his great study *Democracy in America*, might mean equality in servitude as well as equality in freedom.

"I know of only two methods of establishing equality in the political world," Tocqueville wrote. "Rights must be given to every citizen, or none at all to anyone . . . save one, who is the master of all." There was no middle ground "between the sovereignty of all and the absolute power of one man." In his astonishing prediction of 20th-century totalitarian dictatorship, Tocqueville explained how the revolution of equality could lead to the *"Führerprinzip"* and more terrible absolutism than the world had ever known.

But when rights are given to every citizen and the sovereignty of all is established, the problem of leadership takes a new form, becomes more exacting than ever before. It is easy to issue commands and enforce them by the rope and the stake, the concentration camp and the *gulag.* It is much harder to use argument and achievement to overcome opposition and win consent. The Founding Fathers of the United States understood the difficulty. They believed that history had given them the opportunity to decide, as Alexander Hamilton wrote in the first Federalist Paper, whether men are indeed capable of basing government on "reflection and choice, or whether they are forever destined to depend . . . on accident and force."

Government by reflection and choice called for a new style of leadership and a new quality of followership. It required leaders to be responsive to popular concerns, and it required followers to be active and informed participants in the process. Democracy does not eliminate emotion from politics; sometimes it fosters demagoguery; but it is confident that, as the greatest of democratic leaders put it, you cannot fool all of the people all of the time. It measures leadership by results and retires those who overreach or falter or fail.

It is true that in the long run despots are measured by results too. But they can postpone the day of judgment, sometimes indefinitely, and in the meantime they can do infinite harm. It is also true that democracy is no guarantee of virtue and intelligence in government, for the voice of the people is not necessarily the voice of God. But democracy, by assuring the right of opposition, offers built-in resistance to the evils inherent in absolutism. As the theologian Reinhold Niebuhr summed it up, "Man's capacity for justice makes democracy possible, but man's inclination to injustice makes democracy necessary."

A second test for leadership is the end for which power is sought. When leaders have as their goal the supremacy of a master race or the promotion of totalitarian revolution or the acquisition and exploitation of colonies or the protection of greed and privilege or the preservation of personal power, it is likely that their leadership will do little to advance the cause of humanity. When their goal is the abolition of slavery, the liberation of women, the enlargement of opportunity for the poor and powerless, the extension of equal rights to racial minorities, the defense of the freedoms of expression and opposition, it is likely that their leadership will increase the sum of human liberty and welfare.

Leaders have done great harm to the world. They have also conferred great benefits. You will find both sorts in this series. Even "good" leaders must be regarded with a certain wariness. Leaders are not demigods; they put on their trousers one leg after another just like ordinary mortals. No leader is infallible, and every leader needs to be reminded of this at regular intervals. Irreverence irritates leaders but is their salvation. Unquestioning submission corrupts leaders and demeans followers. Making a cult of a leader is always a mistake. Fortunately hero worship generates its own antidote. "Every hero," said Emerson, "becomes a bore at last."

The signal benefit the great leaders confer is to embolden the rest of us to live according to our own best selves, to be active, insistent, and resolute in affirming our own sense of things. For great leaders attest to the reality of human freedom against the supposed inevitabilities of history. And they attest to the wisdom and power that may lie within the most unlikely of us, which is why Abraham Lincoln remains the supreme example of great leadership. A great leader, said Emerson, exhibits new possibilities to all humanity. "We feed on genius. . . . Great men exist that there may be greater men."

Great leaders, in short, justify themselves by emancipating and empowering their followers. So humanity struggles to master its destiny, remembering with Alexis de Tocqueville: "It is true that around every man a fatal circle is traced beyond which he cannot pass; but within the wide verge of that circle he is powerful and free; as it is with man, so with communities."

1

The March on Rome

In October 1922, Italy was in a state of civil war. To millions of Italians, it seemed that their country's days as a constitutional monarchy with a parliamentary system of government were numbered. Throughout the previous four years, the liberal and conservative politicians, who traditionally constituted a majority in Parliament, had shown themselves increasingly incapable of providing effective leadership in the face of rising social tensions and burgeoning economic problems. The crisis brought about by their weakness and incompetence had spawned a new breed of Italian politicians, men who followed a violent and anarchic political credo known as fascism.

The fascists and their followers were militarist authoritarians. Theirs was a politics of action, and they had nothing but contempt for parliamentary democracy. The fascists yearned for the destruction of the old order, for a resurgence of nationalism, and, ultimately, for Italy's transformation into a major world power, for her return to the *grandezza*, or grandeur, she had known 2,000 years before, when Rome, the Italian capital, had been the center of a mighty empire.

Victory should not be mutilated by last-minute concessions. The government must be decidedly Fascist.
—BENITO MUSSOLINI

Benito Mussolini's dictatorship over Italy lasted more than 20 years, from his coming to power as prime minister in 1922 until he was ousted as supreme leader in 1943. His fascist regime became the model for those of Adolf Hitler in Germany, Francisco Franco in Spain, and Juan Perón in Argentina.

Members of Mussolini's fascist militia, the "blackshirts," wave black hats on their bayonets, chanting *"Duce! Duce!"* Ritualistic military displays were an integral part of Mussolini's rule, which was openly based on the ruthless use of absolute power.

The fascists considered violence a legitimate political weapon, and the blood of thousands of socialists and communists—the fascists' bitter enemies—now ran in the streets of Italy's cities and towns every day. The police, most of whom thought the use of violence against leftists acceptable, rarely intervened to stop the slaughter. Always taking care to avoid a fair fight, the fascist *squadri*, or squads, set upon individual socialists and communists, beating them to the ground with *manganelli*, the heavy wooden clubs that had become one of their most conspicuous trademarks. The *squadristi*, as the members of the squadri were known, frequently subjected their victims to humiliation as well as injury, forcibly administering massive, occasionally fatal doses of castor oil, a powerful laxative.

By 1922 the black-shirted fascist squadristi, or "Blackshirts," had taken control of numerous city governments. The leader of the fascist movement, a 39-year-old journalist named Benito Mussolini, was hinting with increasing frequency at the imminence of a "march on Rome." Mussolini intended that his threats, whose vagueness made them all the more ominous, should intimidate the government by suggesting that the fascists could march into Rome and oust the parliamentarians, just as they had thrown out the socialists and communists elsewhere in the country. His intimations were also designed to assist him in consolidating his hold over frequently undisciplined followers. The prospect of a single momentous mass action would, he believed, serve to unite them in a way that the continuation of the present, somewhat disorderly campaign of violence could not. Mussolini also felt that promising such a demonstration would help him undercut the appeal of those among his closest colleagues who might secretly be aspiring to leadership of the Blackshirts.

Mussolini (left) with Italo Balbo in 1933. Balbo, one of four senior fascist leaders poised to carry out Mussolini's threatened coup in October 1922, later served as head of the fascist militia, minister of the air force, and governor of the Italian colony of Libya.

Even as the government plodded along, incapable of ending the violence and equally incapable of governing, thousands of fascists prepared for the event that is known to history as the "March on Rome." The four senior fascists whom Mussolini had appointed to command the march—Italo Balbo, Emilio De Bono, Cesare Maria De Vecchi, and Michele Bianchi—established their headquarters in Perugia, a town about 85 miles north of Rome. Following Italian fascism's policy of imitating ancient Roman political practice, the four men referred to themselves as *quadrumviri*, after the quadrumvirates, or four-man ruling cliques, that had sometimes wielded power over the Roman Empire. Mussolini, for his part, based himself in Milan, a city more than 400 miles from the capital and fairly close to the Swiss border. He wanted to be able to deal with the government from a safe distance, standing above the fray while the marchers exerted pressure on the capital. If the march should turn into a disaster, he calculated, he could be in Switzerland in a matter of hours.

Shortly after 2:00 A.M. on October 28, Italy's King Victor Emmanuel III accepted the recommendation of his cabinet ministers that a state of emergency be declared throughout the kingdom. He also assented to their request that the armed forces, of which he was commander in chief, be employed to impose martial law. During the next few hours, thousands of posters proclaiming martial law were pasted up on walls and billboards all over Rome.

Mussolini reviews his troops in 1922. After three years of violence perpetrated against the left by fascist *squadristi*, he threatened to carry out a "March on Rome" to seize power in October of that year. He oversaw preparations for the march from the safe distance of Milan, well to the north.

under his leadership. The premiership, he said, was the only position he would be willing to accept.

Mussolini had not always been so bold. In recent weeks, he had bargained behind the scenes with a number of politicians, sounding out which of them would make the greatest concessions to him and his party. A few days earlier, he had actually declared himself willing to accept a subordinate position. He changed his mind, however, under pressure from Bianchi, who advised him to abandon all compromise and to increase his demands. Mussolini now realized that the combination of civil chaos and governmental paralysis almost certainly represented the best opportunity to seize power that he would ever have.

On the morning of October 29, Mussolini, seeking to intensify the crisis still further, penned a provocative article in his newspaper, *Il Popolo d'Italia,* or *The People of Italy*:

> This is the situation. The greater part of northern Italy is in the hands of the Fascists. Central Italy . . . is occupied by the Blackshirts. . . . The political authority . . . has not been able to cope with the movement. . . . A tremendous victory is in sight. . . . The government must have a clear Fascist character. Let the men of Rome understand that the hour has come to finish with the old conventional procedures. . . . Let them understand that up to the present moment a solution of the crisis can still be obtained within the framework of the most orthodox constitutionalism, but that tomorrow it may perhaps be too late. . . . Fascism wants power and will have it.

Mussolini thus announced that future deals and compromises would be made on his terms and that all who dared to question those terms risked the brutal attentions of the squadristi. Italian politics had moved from the ornate chambers of Parliament to the streets. The "old conventional procedures" to which Mussolini referred had been superseded by, and would, he intended, find themselves helpless against the political practice of fascism, which entailed the indiscriminate use of guns, knives, grenades, manganelli, and castor oil.

Fascism is not a system of immutable beliefs but a path to political power.
—BENITO MUSSOLINI

Late in the morning of October 29, after the appearance of his article in *Il Popolo d'Italia*, Mussolini received another telephone call from Rome, this time from one of the quadrumviri, who informed him that the king wanted him to come to Rome to assume the premiership and form a government.

Even though it now seemed certain that his campaign of intimidation had paid off, Mussolini wanted tangible proof of the king's intentions. He requested that the offer be confirmed by telegram. When the telegram arrived a short time later, Mussolini decided to leave for Rome that night. He spent the afternoon putting his affairs in order and preparing the next day's edition of *Il Popolo d'Italia*, whose control now passed to his brother Arnaldo. Shortly before leaving Milan, Mussolini ordered the destruction of the offices of two socialist newspapers. He was determined to ensure that no criticisms or strikes should dim the glory of his first days in power.

Arnaldo Mussolini, the Duce's brother, took control of the newspaper *Il Popolo d'Italia* when his brother was called to Rome by Victor Emmanuel III. Benito had founded the paper in 1914 as a mouthpiece for his support of Italy's intervention in World War I.

2

Bad Boy Benito

Benito Mussolini was born outside the village of Predappio, in the northeastern Italian province of Forlì on July 29, 1883. Predappio is situated in a region of Italy known as the Romagna, which, like many areas of the country, had been an international battleground for centuries, plagued by invading armies and subject to a succession of foreign rulers. Some of those rulers had reigned in the name of the Roman Catholic church; others had held power in their own right, usurping the Church's authority. During that period, the people of the region, which was one of the poorest in all Italy, had acquired an enduring reputation as relentless fighters for freedom and independence, repeatedly rising up in revolt against popes and princes alike.

Italy's unification as a nation during the 1860s did little to diminish the rebelliousness of the people of the Romagna. Their opposition to the Roman Catholic church, whose exercise of power prior to its dispossession at the time of unification had often

He [Mussolini] was a boy who did not shed tears and rarely laughed, who spoke little and liked his own company, who preferred reading to playing with others.
—LAURA FERMI
historian

Mussolini depicted as a classroom bully in a 1923 editorial cartoon after he ordered the bombardment and occupation of the Greek island of Corfu. As a child, he was in fact a classroom bully, whose repeated assaults upon schoolmates led to expulsion from his first boarding school.

The Russian anarchist Mikhail Bakunin (1814–76) was a major influence on Mussolini's father, Alessandro, a committed socialist. Bakunin believed that mankind was inherently good and should be granted complete freedom; he supported the violent overthrow of all governments.

been murderously cruel, continued unabated. During the 19th century, many people in the Romagna had come under the influence of anarchism and socialism, political philosophies that addressed the problems of social and economic inequality. This, then, was the tempestuous political and cultural climate of the region where Benito Mussolini grew to manhood.

Benito's mother, Rosa Maltoni, came from a lower-middle-class background. Upon completing her schooling, she qualified for a teaching diploma, and after her marriage she taught elementary school in one of the three rooms of the Mussolini residence. Her upright character and dedication to teaching had made her a respected figure in the community. Rosa was also an extremely devout Catholic. Benito, who rarely formed close personal bonds and found it difficult to express affection, would testify throughout his life that his greatest love was for his mother.

Benito's father, Alessandro, was a blacksmith. He came from a Romagnol peasant family. In distinct contrast to his wife, Alessandro Mussolini was violently anticlerical and a convinced atheist. He was also a committed socialist. His education in radical politics had begun in his late teens, when he encountered the work of the Russian anarchist Mikhail Bakunin, who had visited the Romagna in the course of his travels around Europe.

Alessandro was also influenced by the work of Karl Marx, the 19th-century German economist and political philosopher, whose writings form the basis of modern communist thought. Marx believed that capitalism—the economic system based on private enterprise—contains the seeds of its own destruction and that it must eventually be replaced by communism, a socioeconomic order in which private property is abolished and people live in harmony and equality, without classes or other social divisions. According to the radical thinkers who built upon the foundation that Marx had laid, communism can only be realized following the creation of an intermediate order called socialism, in which the *proletariat*, or working class, owns the means of production—the land and the factories.

Mussolini was born in this house outside the northeast Italian village of Predappio, located in a region known as the Romagna. Until the mid-19th century, the Romagna was controlled by the Papal States, whose harsh rule of the region gave rise to widespread anticlericalism among the Romagnols.

Alessandro Mussolini's strong-minded political views and intolerance for the more inactive "armchair revolutionaries" greatly affected his son Benito, shown here at the age of 14 while attending a secular school in Forlimpopoli.

Marx also held that the transition from capitalism to socialism can only be achieved by revolution, that control of the means of production must be seized by the proletariat from the *bourgeoisie*—the social class defined by Marx's colleague Friedrich Engels as "the class of modern capitalists, owners of the means of social production and employers of wage labor"—because no bourgeois will give up his property willingly in the interests of progress toward a more just and egalitarian social order. Another important element of Marx's teachings was his contention that worldwide communism is historically inevitable because both class war between capitalists and workers *and* the workers' victory over the capitalists are historically inevitable.

Alessandro Mussolini took his socialism very seriously, and he managed to establish connections with many other socialists, both inside Italy and abroad. He set up a local branch of the broad socialist organization known as the Second International of Social Democratic Parties and devoted much of his time, effort, and money to promoting its political views. (The First International had been led by Marx and existed between 1864 and 1876.) Alessandro's commitment to politics seems to have been more profound than his commitment to his smithy, as the family generally had to depend on Rosa's income, which, though small, had the advantage of at least being regular. Indeed, the Mussolinis were better off financially than most of their neighbors.

Benito, whose father had named him after the Mexican revolutionary leader Benito Juárez, would eventually acquire a passion for politics that was as profound as his father's. He would also inherit his father's predilection for socialist/anarchist political activism and his scorn for those more introspective socialists who are sometimes referred to as "armchair revolutionaries." Both Benito and Alessandro had fiery personalities that often found expression in violent behavior and on more than one occasion landed them in jail.

Rosa and Alessandro had two other children in addition to Benito—a son named Arnaldo and a daughter named Edvige. Family ties were not especially close among the children. Mussolini himself said that when his father died in 1910, so did the unity of his family.

As a child, Benito Mussolini was strong-willed, unruly, and violent. He frequently got into fights and felt no compunction about throwing stones at his classmates. On one occasion, he repeatedly struck a playmate with whom he had had an argument, pounding away at the unfortunate child with a sharpened stone and not stopping until he had drawn blood. Benito was also a solitary child. Even in later life, when he was married with a family of his own, kept a string of mistresses, and led a mass political movement, Mussolini remained a loner.

Benito occasionally helped out in his father's smithy. The smithy frequently served as a meeting place for his father's friends or as a refuge for political comrades on the run from the authorities, and it was there that Benito received much of his early exposure to socialism and anticlericalism. In matters of religion, the young Benito was influenced by his mother, who regularly took him to church. Although quite impressed by the symbolism and mysticism of ecclesiastical ritual, Benito soon decided that religion did not particularly interest him.

When Benito reached age nine, his parents decided to send him to a boarding school. Alessandro and Rosa felt that continued schooling would give their son a sense of discipline, broaden his horizons, and improve his prospects of pursuing a good career. In his autobiography, Mussolini hardly mentions his parents' decision, merely noting, "I was about to enter into a period of routine, of learning the ways of the disciplined human herd."

It is not surprising that young Benito, who was already something of a rebel and very much a loner, found life at the boarding school, which was run by a religious order called the Salesians, absolutely unbearable. The regimentation of all activity, the constant and intrusive vigilance of the teachers, and the pronounced lack of privacy made him miserable. He constantly fought with his classmates and came

Mussolini as a boy sought quarrels for their own sake and because he needed to dominate. If he won a bet he asked for more than his due and if he lost he tried to avoid payment.
—I. DEBEGNAC
historian

into conflict with his teachers, who recognized his intelligence but considered him hopelessly unruly. Mussolini once threw an ink pot at a teacher; on another occasion he stabbed a classmate with a pocketknife.

Mussolini's frequent outbursts of violence and unwillingness to accept discipline eventually persuaded his teachers that they had no choice but to expel him. He was asked to leave the school at the end of his second year there. A few months later, his parents enrolled him in a secular school, the Royal Normal School at Forlimpopoli, a town about 10 miles from Predappio.

Mussolini found the regimen at the Royal Normal School much more humane than the one he had experienced at the Salesian school. Although his vindictiveness and unwillingness to submit to discipline remained a problem, his teachers showed great patience, and the young man made considerable academic progress. In his personal life during this period, Mussolini emerged as something of an eccentric, as someone who was determined to stand out from the crowd and emphasize his individuality. He took to sporting a long, flowing black scarf, exhibiting a flamboyance and an eagerness to draw attention to himself that were unusual in a country boy from the Romagna.

During the seven years that he spent at the Royal Normal School, Mussolini became increasingly interested in politics. Visiting home on weekends, he discussed politics with his father and read the leaflets and newspapers his father's socialist friends brought with them. He took the ideas that he learned at home back to school with him and regularly harangued his classmates with speeches on the virtues of socialism and the injustices visited on working people under capitalism. He thus began to acquire a certain proficiency at public speaking. He also began to write political articles.

In 1901, Mussolini graduated from the Royal Normal School with a teaching diploma and a solid, if undistinguished, academic record. Shortly before his graduation, he was chosen by the headmaster to speak at a public ceremony in honor of the great

> *I came from a lineage of honest people. They tilled the soil.*
> —BENITO MUSSOLINI

3

Young Radical

After receiving his teaching diploma, Mussolini taught elementary school for a few months in 1902 in Gualtieri, a small town near Predappio. Although he quite enjoyed life in Gualtieri, he did not develop any great inclination to stay there. He found his income too small, the tenor of the town more provincial than was strictly to his liking, and the local socialists insufficiently revolutionary. Even at this early stage of his political development, in fact, Mussolini had begun to exhibit the hostility to moderation in politics that would distinguish him throughout his life.

At that time, Italian socialism contained two main schools of thought. On one side, and very much in a minority within the movement, were the anarchists and the *internazionalisti*, or internationalists. Neither the anarchists nor the internazionalisti were above resorting to violence and subversion. The internazionalisti, with whom the young Mussolini increasingly identified, rejected patriotism as a bourgeois emotion and never viewed the struggle to achieve socialism in Italy in isolation from the broader effort to realize socialism worldwide. The other school of Italian socialist thought, and the one

> *I feel the wanderlust in my blood, pushing me on. I am a restless man, a wild temperament, shy of popularity.*
> —BENITO MUSSOLINI

In the early years of the 20th century, Italian socialists sought to improve working conditions among the nation's impoverished peasants and industrial laborers. Mussolini would begin his political career as a radical socialist, advocating the use of violence to achieve those ends.

In 1902, Mussolini moved to Lausanne, Switzerland, possibly to avoid the draft. His emerging socialist convictions at this time were inconsistent with most of his later fascist doctrines. He left Switzerland late in 1904.

in the majority, believed in using legal methods to advance the socialist cause. It favored agitating for social reforms that would improve working conditions in industry and generally increase the workers' standard of living.

The more revolutionary, minority members of the PSI identified themselves with the party's "maximum program," which advocated the intensification of class struggle, the socialization of the means of production, and political independence from bourgeois liberalism and reformism. The more moderate, mainstream members of the PSI identified themselves with the party's "minimum program," which called for universal suffrage for both sexes, proportional representation, nationalization of transport and mines, and the establishment of a free, strictly secular educational system.

The PSI's official platform was the minimum program; but in adopting it, the party was not turning its back on the maximum program, which the PSI leaders pointedly defined as "the compass by which the party should keep its direction." Mussolini himself, throughout his career as a socialist, would become increasingly closely identified with the *massimalisti*, as the devotees of the maximum program were known. And as he came to prominence within the movement, his personal tendency toward extremism would, at one and the same time, sow the seeds of fascism and help imbue Italian left-wing radicalism with a confrontational quality that it has retained to this day.

When his temporary schoolteaching job ended in June 1902, Mussolini went to Lausanne, Switzerland. There, he had no money, no place to stay, and few prospects of finding well-paid employment. After a few days, he got a job as a construction laborer, but finding hard work distinctly disagreeable, he quit after a week. At one time, hunger and despair brought him to the brink of suicide. Penniless, Mussolini resorted to begging and on some nights slept under a bridge. After being arrested for vagrancy and thrown into jail for three days, he decided that his habitual need for solitude would have to be subordinated to his more immediate need simply to survive. Accordingly, he sought out other socialists among the Italian community in Lausanne.

Mussolini's new acquaintances helped him find a number of menial jobs, none of which he liked or kept for very long, and he soon began spending much of his time writing articles for socialist newspapers. He also spoke regularly at political meetings and on one occasion helped organize a masons' strike. These activities not only won Mussolini a degree of renown in socialist circles but got him into trouble with the authorities; they responded to his agitation among Switzerland's Italian immigrant workers, who were vital to the country's hotel and tourism industry, with short jail terms and expulsions from one administrative district to another. Finally, in July 1903, he was expelled from Switzerland, but managed to slip back into the country by the end of the year.

Mussolini at age 22. The Russian socialist Angelica Balabanoff, a close associate of Mussolini during his days as a socialist, later described him as a man whose political convictions arose from a passion "to assert his own ego and from a determination for personal revenge."

During the two years that Mussolini spent in Switzerland, his political consciousness continued to mature. His writings and speeches were characterized by extremism and calls for violent action. Mussolini showed very little interest in theorizing or moderation. This attitude led to his being considered by many observers as more of an anarchist than a socialist. There was, indeed, much about Mussolini's thought that reflected the strong anarchist influence of the political culture of the Romagna.

Mussolini's writings from this period reveal that his anticlericalism had survived his departure from the Romagna. Some of his most bitter comments were reserved for fellow socialists who remained devout Catholics. He had also become a violent antimonarchist, regularly reviling kings as ignorant and reactionary and demanding that Italy be reconstituted as a republic. Mussolini's antimonarchism and anticlericalism were supplemented by an intense antimilitarism. He abhorred the fact that the monarchy sometimes used the military to suppress popular agitation, and he disapproved of the armed forces' blind obedience to their political masters. He also took the standard internationalist view of patriotism as a bourgeois conceit that served only to strengthen militarism and to reinforce the state at the expense of the workers. Mussolini believed that young men, instead of supporting the army by paying taxes and being patriotic, should register their opposition to militarism by refusing to be conscripted or, if they were already in the army, by deserting.

During this period, Mussolini also began to make useful political contacts. One person who influenced him considerably was Angelica Balabanoff, who, like Mussolini, was a foreigner in Switzerland. She came from a well-to-do Russian family and had traveled to western Europe to further her education. Balabanoff was a member of the Russian social-democratic, or Marxian socialist, movement, and her socialism was a good deal more sophisticated than Mussolini's. The young Italian learned much about politics from Balabanoff, and he revealed more of himself to her than he did to his other comrades. From Balabanoff's writings, we gain some insight into Mussolini's personality at this time: In *My Life as a Rebel*, she writes:

> I soon saw that he knew little of history, of economics, or of Socialist theory and that his mind was completely undisciplined. . . . Mussolini's radicalism and anticlericalism were more the reflection of his early environment and his own rebellious egoism than the product of understanding and conviction; his hatred of oppression was not that impersonal hatred of a system shared by all revolutionaries; it sprang rather from his own sense of indignity and frustration, from a passion to assert his own ego and from a determination for personal revenge.

The lack of conviction that Balabanoff discusses was very much in evidence in Mussolini's actions in November 1904, when he decided to go back to Italy. It is possible that one of Mussolini's reasons for going to Switzerland in the first place was to avoid being drafted into the Italian army. During

Mussolini would be ill dressed, dirty and unshaven in public, as befitted a proletarian leader, and then [he would] quickly change to absurd, overstylish, patent leather shoes and silk-lapelled coat for his private life.
—LEDA RAFANELLI
socialist and Mussolini
acquaintance

the course of his stay in Switzerland, Mussolini had in fact become a draft dodger; men of his age had been due to report for training in January 1904. In late 1904, however, Victor Emmanuel III proclaimed an amnesty for deserters, and Mussolini, the self-professed antimilitarist, took advantage of this opportunity to return to Italy and join the army.

Despite his antimilitarism, Mussolini accepted the authority of his superiors and temporarily abandoned his political activities. After his discharge in 1906, he returned to a life of uncertainty. Unable to come up with any viable alternatives, he fell back on his qualifications and again taught school. In 1908, Mussolini moved to Oneglia, a small city on the Italian Riviera, where he worked as the editor of a socialist periodical. In 1909, he received an invitation to become secretary of the chamber of labor (a socialist center for trade unions) in Trent, the capital of the Austrian province of Trentino, and to edit a socialist weekly there. The Trentino, traditionally Italian in culture and language but at that time under Austrian control, was part of what the Italians referred to as *Italia irredenta*, or "unredeemed Italy"—former Italian territories lost to Italian rule due to the aggression of foreign powers. The other regions classified as Italia irredenta were the South Tyrol, Istria, Gorizia, Gradisca, and Trieste.

In Trent, Mussolini was able to increase his reputation and develop his skills as a political journalist. After six months with the chamber of labor, he found a new job, becoming subeditor of a daily newspaper that was committed to the cause of bringing Italia irredenta back under Italian control. In his writings at this time, Mussolini promoted his anticlerical and revolutionary socialist views. It is also possible that it was as a result of working at the irredentist newspaper that Mussolini now began to pay some attention to the nationalist viewpoint. (Mussolini's Marxist internationalism was, however, to remain pronounced for several more years.) He was frequently fined and thrown into jail because of the inflammatory, and occasionally libelous, statements he made in his articles. In September 1909, just eight months after he had arrived, Mussolini was expelled from the Trentino.

The expulsion enhanced Mussolini's growing prestige among Italian socialists. Shortly after he went back to Italy, he was offered the position of political organizer of the socialist clubs in Forlì. There he edited a socialist weekly newspaper, using his position to denounce the parliamentary system and to demand revolutionary action. This brought him into conflict not only with republicans but also with the moderate, reformist members of his own party. Yet Mussolini did not put forth any clear views of where the revolutionary action for which he called was to lead.

Mussolini also used his newspaper to publicize his antimilitarism, and in 1911 he came out strongly against the Italian government's decision to invade and colonize Libya, which at that time was part of the Ottoman Turkish Empire. Italy already had two colonies, Eritrea and Somalia, in Africa, but Prime Minister Giovanni Giolitti and his colleagues in the government hoped that yet another military adventure would raise Italy to new heights of grandezza and bring her closer to parity

The Romagna was a poor rural region known for the strong socialist and anarchist sentiments of its inhabitants. The Mussolinis were far from wealthy, but they were better off financially than most Romagnols and led a relatively comfortable existence.

In 1911–12, under Prime Minister Giovanni Giolitti, Italy fought a brutal colonial war to conquer Libya. Mussolini, at this point still an ardent antimilitarist, vehemently condemned the war. He was jailed for inciting acts of vandalism aimed at slowing the war effort.

with Great Britain and France, the two leading imperial powers in Africa.

Mussolini's recommendations for opposing the war with Turkey included calling a general strike and encouraging the workers to carry out sabotage and resistance. Partly as a result of his agitation, riots erupted in Forlì, and troops were called in to restore order. Mussolini was arrested, tried, and sentenced to five months in prison.

Mussolini emerged from prison to find his prestige still further on the increase. His own aspirations had also become much greater. The next significant step in his political career occurred just four months later, in July 1912, when he made an appearance at a national congress of the PSI in the town of Reggio Emilia. At the congress, Mussolini presented himself as a maximalist and acted as a spokesman for a new, hard-left tendency within the party whose members were known as "intransigents." He gave a speech attacking the moderates, many of whom had actually supported the annexation of Libya, and proposed that four of the most prominent moderate reformists be expelled from the party, including their leader, Leonida Bissolati, and a future prime minister named Ivanoe Bonomi. When he finished speaking, he was given a massive ovation. Mussolini had now achieved his first oratorical success at the national level.

The congress accepted Mussolini's proposal, and the four reformists were expelled from the party. Mussolini, along with Balabanoff and several other revolutionaries, was then elected to the party's executive committee. He was now a member of the hierarchy of one of Italy's leading political parties. In December, Mussolini rose to new heights of authority and influence when the party leadership appointed him editor of the PSI's official daily newspaper, *Avanti!*.

As editor of *Avanti!*, Mussolini had to adhere more closely to official party policy than he had before. In fact, one of the party leaders who voted against Mussolini's appointment as editor did so because he considered Mussolini too much of an individualist to be entrusted with such an important party po-

Austrian archduke Franz Ferdinand, shown here with his daughter, was assassinated in June 1914 by the Serbian nationalist Gavrilo Princip, starting the series of events that within weeks led to the outbreak of World War I. Italy remained neutral until May 1915, when it declared war on Austria.

Most European socialists responded to the outbreak of war in a manner that made a mockery of the Second International's resolution calling on socialist parties everywhere to work to prevent conflict, or, if war broke out, to demand its immediate cessation. On August 4, 1914, the German Social Democratic party, the largest and most influential of the Second International's affiliated parties, became the first party to defy the resolution when its parliamentary representatives voted to approve the German government's request for war credits. A fatal example had been set, and the leaders of the socialist parties in the other belligerent countries lined up behind their national rulers, telling the workers they represented to fight and die as patriots.

In Italy, which was not among the belligerent nations, Mussolini had unhesitatingly promoted the internationalist line. The headline of the July 26, 1914, edition of *Avanti!* read: "Let a single cry arise from the vast multitudes of the proletariat, and let it be repeated in the squares and streets of Italy: Down with the War."

4

"War on Socialism"

Italy stayed neutral in the conflict until several months after its outbreak. The social groups that favored neutrality were the liberals, conservatives, members of the Catholic party, and industrialists whose enterprises depended on German financial backing. Prime Minister Giolitti and his supporters were also in favor of neutrality; they had taken careful note of the organizational shortcomings and material deficiencies that had plagued the army during the Libyan campaign and clearly recognized that Italy was in no position to fight a war. Giolitti and his fellow neutralists in Parliament faced considerable opposition, however, from an increasingly vociferous coalition of nationalists, republicans, and irredentists. Two months after the outbreak of war, Mussolini himself defected to the pro-war grouping.

Rather than having his editorials reflect party policy, Mussolini now began using *Avanti!* as a vehicle for his own views, passing them off as party policy. He asked the Italian socialists if they wanted to be protagonists in the war or mere bystanders. Mussolini did not discuss his change of views with anyone, not even with Balabanoff, his closest colleague

A victorious Germany will turn Italy into a desert peopled by slaves.
—BENITO MUSSOLINI

In World War I, Mussolini fought in the trenches on the Italian-Austrian front, where he was eventually promoted from the rank of private to that of corporal. More than 650,000 Italians were killed in the war, most of them in the fighting against Austria.

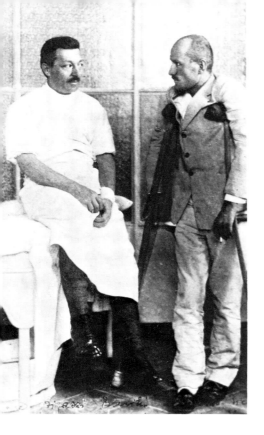

During a routine training exercise in February 1917, Mussolini (right) was wounded when a grenade thrower he was operating blew up. After four months in the hospital, he was discharged from military service. He returned to civilian life as editor of his newspaper *Il Popolo d'Italia*.

for more than 10 years. In mid-October, there was a stormy meeting of the PSI's executive committee. When asked for an explanation of his *volte-faccia*, or "about-face," Mussolini said nothing. He was forced by the committee to resign his editorship of *Avanti!*.

Mussolini took this latest development in stride. Within four weeks, the first edition of Mussolini's answer to *Avanti!*, a publication called *Il Popolo d'Italia*, or *The People of Italy*, appeared on the streets. Backed by money from France, Britain, and other nations allied against Germany and Austria-Hungary, and receiving further financing from Italian industrialists and arms manufacturers, it included an editorial in which Mussolini said, "My cry is a fearful and fascinating word: *War!*"

Soon thereafter, another meeting of the executive committee was held. Amid shouts and jeers Mussolini was expelled from the party. Although he said he still considered himself a socialist, this was the juncture of his definitive break with the PSI. The hatred of socialism and the scorn for former comrades that Mussolini now began to nurse would stay with him for the rest of his life. And yet the disturbing new politics that he now began to formulate would be strikingly similar, in terms of its shortcomings, to that which the "intransigent" socialists had practiced. Incoherence, hatred of reformism, and relentless hostility to parliamentary democracy were all to be hallmarks of fascism.

Thinking that the war would not last long and fearful of losing an opportunity to share in the spoils of victory, Italy entered the war on May 24, 1915, on the side of the Allied powers—France, Great Britain, and Russia. Popular support for intervention in the conflict had become so strong that the Giolittians could no longer maintain their majority in Parliament. Prior to the declaration of war, Italy's new prime minister, a conservative named Antonio Salandra, had negotiated a secret treaty with the Allies whereby Italy, once the Allied powers had beaten Germany and Austria, would receive ports and islands in the Adriatic and the eastern Mediterranean, territory in Africa, concessions in the

Balkans, and several areas that currently fell within Italia irredenta—the Trentino, Trieste, and Istria.

Mussolini's advocacy of interventionism undoubtedly had some effect on Italian public opinion, but the main impetus in moving popular sentiment toward intervention was provided by the increasingly powerful nationalist movement, whose most influential figure was an extremely popular poet, playwright, and novelist named Gabriele D'Annunzio. D'Annunzio's work and the speeches he gave glorified sensuality, belittled spirituality, and encouraged his country to strive for grandezza. The speeches D'Annunzio gave to a wide variety of audiences in May 1915 were in large part responsible for the downfall of the neutralists.

Mussolini, despite his exhortations in favor of Italy's entrance into the war, did not volunteer for military service. He was eventually conscripted in September 1915. In the first months after he was called up, however, Mussolini did not see much action. In November, he fell ill and was given sick leave.

While he was on leave, Mussolini took care of a number of personal matters. For about five years he had been living with a woman named Rachele Guidi, and Mussolini now married her. In 1910, Rachele had given birth to their first child, a girl they named Edda, and in September 1915 she gave birth to a second child, a boy whom they named Vittorio. At the same time, one of Mussolini's many mistresses informed him that she, too, had just given birth to a son of his. Mussolini formally recognized the child as his own.

Mussolini returned to the Italian-Austrian front, which had stabilized along the Isonzo River in northern Italy, in February 1916. In February 1917 he was wounded during a training exercise. The grenade thrower that he was operating overheated and blew up, peppering Mussolini with shrapnel and killing several bystanders. Mussolini spent four months in a hospital and was then discharged from the army. He returned to his desk at *Il Popolo d'Italia.*

World War I ended in an Allied victory with the armistice of November 11, 1918. Diplomats from

> *I ask for ferocious men — I ask for one ferocious man with energy, with the energy to tear apart, with the inflexibility to punish and strike without hesitation — and so much the better if the culprit is in a high position.*
> —BENITO MUSSOLINI

Mussolini (left) with the Italian poet, nationalist, and soldier Gabriele D'Annunzio. A hero as a pilot in World War I, D'Annunzio would become an early fascist icon after he led a successful coup to take Fiume, a city disputed by Italy and Yugoslavia, and set up a dictatorial regime there in 1919.

the Allied nations—with the exception of Russia, where communist revolutionaries led by Vladimir Ilich Lenin, Marx's most influential intellectual disciple, had seized power in November 1917 and signed a separate peace with Germany in March 1918—met with their counterparts from Germany and her allies in Paris in January 1919 to negotiate the terms of a final peace settlement.

The Italian armed forces, like those of all the other belligerent nations, had sustained appalling casualties during the war. More than 650,000 Italian troops had been killed, and a further 500,000 had been wounded. The younger veterans had grown from boyhood to manhood during the conflict, and many of them found it extraordinarily difficult to adapt to civilian life.

Not only did the soldiers come back as different people, but the Italy to which they returned had changed dramatically, as well. For Italian industry and commerce, readjusting to peacetime conditions proved extremely problematic. Shortages of financing, of raw materials, and of export markets caused severe constraints. Jobs were scarce and pay was low.

In the postwar peace negotiations, many of the Italian claims to which Great Britain and France had agreed in 1915 were ignored. This was mainly the result of the position taken by the government of the United States, which had entered the war on the side of the Allies in 1917. U.S. president Woodrow Wilson was determined to achieve a peace settlement that involved as few territorial gains and losses as possible, and his unusually high-minded and moralistic approach to politics made him particularly averse to claims contained in secret treaties.

As the Paris Peace Conference progressed throughout 1919, many Italians came to feel that their country was being treated as if it had been on the losing side. Under the terms of the Treaty of St. Germain, which was signed on September 10, 1919, and constituted a final settlement between the Allies and Austria, Italy finally gained control of the Trentino, Istria, and the South Tyrol. Later negotiations yielded minor territorial gains in Africa. All these gains, however, were far less than Italy had originally hoped to realize.

Particularly aggravating to many Italians was the lack of good faith shown by Great Britain and France following the creation at the Paris Peace Conference of the League of Nations, an organization that was intended to preserve peace and settle disputes by arbitration. It was agreed that former German colonies in Africa, as well as those of Turkey (which had sided with Germany in the war), would be administered by the Allied nations under League "mandates," or commissions to govern. The leaders of the Italian delegation briefly went to Rome to consult with their government, but when they returned they discovered that the allocation of mandates in Africa and the Middle East had been made in their absence. Under the allocation, Great Britain and France vastly increased their overseas territories. Italy got nothing.

It was in response to this political and diplomatic debacle that D'Annunzio coined the phrase of Italy's "mutilated victory." Mussolini and many other extreme nationalists quickly seized upon this phrase and used it to whip up much patriotic indignation.

Bolshevik guards prepare for fighting in Russia's October Revolution in 1917, which resulted in the formation of the Soviet Union, the world's first communist state. Fear among European governments of similar revolutions helped pave the way for acceptance of anticommunist movements of the extreme right.

The years immediately following the war saw immense political turmoil in Italy. Many veterans wanted to tear down the old order, which had consigned them first to the horrors of war and then to the privations of existence under a shattered economy and widespread unemployment. After the frightening experience of war, many men proved willing to undertake extraordinary actions in order to bring about a different world. But just like Mussolini, a large proportion of these activists had no clear idea of what kind of world they wanted to build in place of the old one. There was also a growing political polarization between the right and the left. Tensions were on the rise.

At the same time, many European socialists were now looking for their inspiration to the workers' state that Lenin and his colleagues were attempting to create in Soviet Russia. Lenin himself was also working hard to intensify the polarization of European politics. At the beginning of 1919, he convened the First Congress of the Third (Communist) International, or Comintern, an organization dedicated to the overthrow of capitalism throughout the world. The Comintern was intended to be a truly revolutionary and insurrectionary organization, exhibiting none of the reformism and moderation that had characterized its predecessor, the Second International. The Comintern's program was designed to split the European socialist parties, separating the revolutionaries from the reformists and reconstituting the revolutionary factions as communist parties.

During this period, Mussolini was moving further to the political right, although his confused philosophy still contained many vaguely socialistic ideas. And it must be stressed that Mussolini's rightism had little in common with traditional conservatism. In fact, Mussolini had as much contempt for conservative politicians as he did for liberals.

In February 1919 one of the first communist demonstrations to take place in Italy was staged in Milan. In reaction, Mussolini held a meeting in Milan on March 23 to found a new organization, the *Fascio Italiana di Combattimento*, the Italian Combat Band. (The word *fascio*, in this context meaning a small, tightly knit group, is derived from the Latin *fasces*—the bundles of rods, from which an ax protruded, that were carried by officials who attended the magistrates of ancient Rome. They symbolized the power to scourge and decapitate.) With this, the fascist movement came into existence.

Fascism was something new. It emerged from the social dislocations that followed the war, from nationalist resentment of the settlements concluded at the Paris Peace Conference, and from middle-class fears that the working class was poised to make a bid for political supremacy.

The men present at the founding of the fascist movement pledged themselves to supporting the claims of all veterans, to opposing imperialism, and to sabotaging the candidacy of any politician who had tried to prevent Italy from joining the war. Also in a speech that he gave at the meeting, Mussolini stated: "We declare war on Socialism." This last policy was perhaps the least ambiguous element of the fascists' proposals.

On several subsequent occasions, Mussolini admitted that fascism had no definite program. Underlining his fascination with action, at one point he remarked, "Fascism was not the nursling of a doctrine worked out beforehand with detailed elaboration; it was born of the need for action and it was itself from the beginning practical rather than theoretical." On another occasion, he testified to the confused and inconsistent nature of fascist ideology: "We allow ourselves the luxury of being

U.S. president Woodrow Wilson (in light coat) examines the ruins of the destroyed cloth hall in Ypres, Belgium, in June 1919. His opposition to the wholesale reapportionment of Europe at the postwar Paris Peace Conference was a factor in leaving Italy with only minor territorial gains.

aristocratic and democratic, reactionary and revolutionary, legalistic and illegalistic, according to the circumstances of place, time, and environment in which we are compelled to live and act."

Mussolini was an opportunist, and his opportunism was nowhere more evident than in his attitude toward the working class and socialism. Although he had "declared war on Socialism," a fascist program that was published a few months later still contained many socialistic elements. A major reason for including such ideas in this program was to entice workers away from the PSI.

The founding meeting of the fascist movement was attended by a remarkably diverse group of individuals, ranging from extreme-right authoritarians through traditional centrists to extreme-left anarchists. Thus it is not surprising that fascism was a hodgepodge of contradictory ideas. Among those in attendance were several members of a movement known as the *arditi*, or daring men, a loose association containing both disaffected veterans and young men who were eager for action because the war had ended before they were old enough to be called up. Also present at the meeting were a number of army officers and a motley collec-

D'Annunzio inspects his troops shortly after his September 1919 takeover of Fiume. Unopposed by the Italian and Yugoslavian governments, he established an independent dictatorship that would serve as a model for Mussolini's future dictatorial rule over Italy.

tion of former socialists, anarchists, republicans, libertarians, and conservatives. Another, and particularly important group, led by poet and writer Filippo Marinetti, were the Futurists, avant-garde artists who worshiped technology, action, revolt, and power.

On April 15, 1919, the fascists conducted what they referred to as their first "punitive expedition." That day, the socialists were holding a rally in Milan. The fascists attacked the demonstrators, dispersed the rally, and then moved on to the offices of *Avanti!*, Mussolini's old paper, where they destroyed the printing equipment and list of subscribers.

The elections of November 1919 gave the PSI 156 of the 535 seats available in the Chamber of Deputies (the lower house of the Italian Parliament), while the fascists failed to gain even a single seat. It was the socialists' best electoral performance ever, and it made the PSI the largest single-party bloc in Parliament. The size of the party's victory, coupled with its revolutionary rhetoric, frightened the country's upper- and middle-class conservatives.

Soon after the elections, Mussolini and about 100 other fascists were arrested for illegal arms possession. They were released the next day—the first sign of a continuing pattern in which the authorities would tolerate fascist squads as long as they were arrayed against the socialists. Still, the fascists were close to disbanding, their dismal showing in the elections making their status as a small splinter group painfully obvious.

But something was already happening that would provide Mussolini with an example of how to proceed. In September 1919, D'Annunzio, who had distinguished himself as a singularly daring bomber pilot during the war and was now more of a national hero than ever, led a group of arditi and some army and navy units that had mutinied into the city of Fiume. Fiume is situated on the Adriatic Sea in what is now Yugoslavia; at that time, it was still one of the "unredeemed" territories. Its status had not been revised at the Paris Peace Conference. D'Annunzio occupied the city and established himself as dictator.

> *Punching is an exquisitely Fascist means of self-expression.*
> —BENITO MUSSOLINI

D'Annunzio's regime in Fiume lasted 15 months. Initially, Mussolini was cautious about D'Annunzio's activities, but eventually he expressed his support. He spoke approvingly of D'Annunzio's coup throughout the fascist election campaign of November 1919, and he also visited Fiume for a day to confer with D'Annunzio. It was during their meeting that the idea of staging a march on Rome was first mentioned.

In light of the fascists' complete failure at the polls, D'Annunzio's success in taking Fiume convinced Mussolini that direct, militant action was not only possible but fruitful. Furthermore, D'Annunzio was an extreme rightist, and although Mussolini was still using the rhetoric of the left, he now saw that right-wing politics represented his best opportunity for gaining power. Most of the major features of D'Annunzio's dictatorship would be incorporated into Mussolini's fascism: the parades, the uniforms, the mysticism, the rallies and meetings staged for maximum dramatic effect, the stress on absolute dictatorship, the revival of Roman symbolism and political terminology, the improvisation and incoherency, and the violence. It was on D'Annunzio's brutal dictatorship that Mussolini would model his own.

In time, enthusiasm for D'Annunzio's initiative began to wane. In November 1920 the Italian and Yugoslav governments signed a temporary bilateral agreement making Fiume an independent state, and on December 24, 1920, Italian troops moved in to expel D'Annunzio and his followers, who offered only minimal resistance. By this point, Mussolini's support for D'Annunzio had also petered out. He had no desire to weaken his own movement by tying it to a losing cause. Mussolini also realized that if he backed D'Annunzio he would undermine his own plan for achieving dictatorial power.

Meanwhile, the government continued to give tacit approval to fascist squads to attack leftists with absolute impunity. Throughout much of 1920, Italy's workers had staged a massive occupation of the factories. Although the occupation movement failed to win the workers any gains, it succeeded in

frightening a majority of middle-class politicians and their capitalist supporters. From that point on, centrist and right-wing fear of communism became a dominant feature of Italian political life. Factory owners and landowners now supported and even bankrolled the "punitive expeditions" of the squadristi against workers, socialists, and communists. Hundreds of fasci sprang up throughout the country. From this time on the army and the police did not interfere with the violence carried out by the fascists.

From the low point after the November 1919 elections, the fascists now quickly gained strength. Giolitti, who was now prime minister again, invited the fascists to join his coalition in the spring of 1921, and Mussolini accepted. In the elections that followed, the fascists won 35 seats. Middle-class politicians now openly supported the antisocialist policies of the fascists. The authorities began providing the squadri with money and weapons and protected them despite their involvement in arson and murder. Such was the climate of government-sanctioned violence that gave rise to the March on Rome.

Fascist blackshirts in Fiume show their support for D'Annunzio's regime. Mussolini, who founded the Fascist party in March 1919, backed D'Annunzio at first. But by December 1920, when the Italian government ejected D'Annunzio and his supporters from Fiume, Mussolini's support had waned.

5

The Fascist State

The March on Rome became the central myth of the founding of the fascist state. In fact, however, no such march actually took place. The fascist squadri did not parade in Rome until after Mussolini had been asked to form a government. The March on Rome was, in essence, a bluff. To defeat the fascists, the government could simply have upheld the constitution and called out the army, which was perfectly capable of crushing the fascists. It also seems certain that if the government had given clear orders, the army would have obeyed. Much of the responsibility for the rise to power of Italian fascism rests, therefore, with the middle-class politicians, who either believed the fascists would "save Italy from socialism" or lacked the courage to oppose them.

Following Mussolini's accession to power, it seemed at first that he would exercise moderation and play by the parliamentary rules. Only four of the fourteen ministers in the first government Mussolini formed were fascists. But in his first speech to Parliament, Mussolini made it clear that if Parliament proved uncooperative, he would dissolve it.

> *Invention is more useful than the truth.*
> —BENITO MUSSOLINI

From the balcony of the Palazzo Venezia in Rome, Mussolini observes the induction of 250,000 recruits into the fascist militia in 1930. *Il Duce*, as he was by now called, survived an early governmental crisis to consolidate his power as dictator in January 1925.

Mussolini is met by supporters in Rome on October 30, 1922. The so-called March on Rome of October 28 was a myth later propagated by the fascists; in reality, the army and police easily prevented the blackshirts from entering the capital. Mussolini arrived on October 30 at the invitation of the king.

Faced with what amounted to an ultimatum and anxious for strong leadership that would protect the interests of the ruling class, Parliament unhesitatingly voted him full powers to make changes in the law. Only the communists and socialists voted against the measure.

Mussolini moved to consolidate his position as quickly as possible. Police officials were replaced with fascists. A new militia was created from the squadri and placed on the government payroll. More opposition newspaper offices were sacked. Convicted criminals were released from prison and recruited to head intimidation squads. During the next 12 months, the squadri committed 2,000 acts of murder, arson, and assault. Through official amnesties and judicial pardons, squadristi went unpunished and were able to proceed without fear of intervention by the police or prosecution by the courts. PSI offices and the homes of opposition politicians were prime targets of the fascist terror campaign. Nothing and nobody would be allowed to stand in Mussolini's way.

Many fascists simply could not believe that Mussolini had allowed such a crisis to develop and continue just because of a political murder; they urged even more overt political violence. Other fascists called for a return to a "normalized" parliamentary government. Mussolini was caught between the boycotting opposition deputies, who denounced him for the violence of his followers, and the fascists, who started to desert him either because of his excessive brutality or because he was not brutal enough. Mussolini's position was eroding dangerously.

By the end of the year, as the liberals and members of the Catholic party joined the boycott, Mussolini's mind was finally made up. The affair had gone on long enough and represented a grave threat to his power. On January 3, 1925, Mussolini delivered a speech in Parliament in which he accepted full responsibility for what had happened. If the deputies dared, he taunted them, they could impeach him. But with the opposition boycotting the session, the only members left in Parliament were the fascists and those conservatives and nationalists who supported him; furthermore, he felt no threat from Victor Emmanuel III, who had already refused to exercise his right to remove Mussolini from the premiership for lacking a parliamentary consensus. Emboldened by the lack of opposition, Mussolini announced he was assuming full dictatorial powers.

Mussolini inspects the fascist militia as they hail their leader. In December 1922, the fascist squadristi were put on the government budget and reorganized as the militia. They continued to act as goon squads, assassination teams, and secret police.

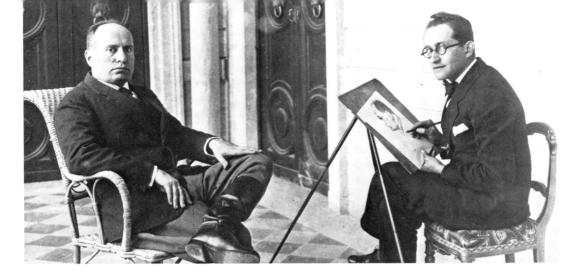

A New York artist begins a portrait of Mussolini in 1927. By now Mussolini virtually controlled all forms of art and creative expression in Italy. Government censors were instructed not to allow the publication of any photo that showed him smiling; all Italians were to follow the Duce's example and be "serious-minded."

His speech had signaled the demise of any pretense to democratic rule, ushering in the end of free speech, a free press, and all toleration of opposition. The fascist militia was mobilized. Political parties and organizations were closed down and outlawed. Newspapers were closed down, bought, or voluntarily went under fascist control. As for those accused of the murder of Matteotti, all were either released before trial, acquitted, or given short jail terms.

Remembering the desertion of some fascists during the Matteotti affair, Mussolini undertook to wipe out any independence among them. The fascist party was purged of those whom Mussolini deemed unreliable and rigidly centralized under his control. Local fascist leaders were dismissed and replaced with new men appointed from Rome. The fascist organization was now established as a strict hierarchy, with Mussolini standing alone at the top. All fascists and fascist militiamen had to swear an oath of allegiance to Mussolini, the infallible *Duce*, or leader, of fascism.

By the end of 1925, all effective opposition had been silenced, Parliament had been reduced to mere symbolic status, and all sectors of the government and the judicial system were brought under Mussolini's direct control. The dictatorship was in place, and the state was reorganized to become an instrument of the will of the fascist party and thus Mussolini himself. Now, all facets of Italian life were to be controlled by the Duce.

the robustness of the nation's birthrate. Mussolini himself had five children, and his wife, Rachele, was duly loyal and deferred to him on all matters. But throughout his life the Duce kept many mistresses—a practice not entirely in opposition to the fascist ideal—among whom his favorite was Clara Petacci, whom he met in 1933.

One of Mussolini's greatest assets was his skill as an actor, his ability to present fascism to the Italians as a living drama. At no time was his theatrical ability shown to better effect than on those occasions when he addressed a crowd from the balcony of the Palazzo Venezia. He would wait in his office until the crowd outside had whipped itself up into a frenzy, and then, while they were still chanting, "Duce! Duce! Duce!," he would stride out onto the balcony, still their shouts with a single glance, thrust his chin forward, and start his harangue.

Mussolini took great care to control all information about his personal life. His office sent daily instructions to the press. Because of his fetish with youth, there was to be no mention of his age, his

In imitation of the legendary figure of Romulus, who outlined the boundaries of ancient Rome with a plow, Mussolini outlines the boundaries of the new model city of Aprilia with a tractor. Mussolini called for the construction of a number of model cities, but few were actually built.

grandchildren, or his birthday. Nothing was to be said about his ulcers or about the fact that he had poor eyesight. Because all Italians were to be "serious-minded," no pictures were to be printed that showed him smiling. Newspapers were told whether or not they could comment on his speeches, and if they could, they were told what to say. In case the people should ever doubt it, "Mussolini is always right" was written on buildings all over the country.

Looming over all these new features of Italian society under fascism was the constant, overarching presence of militarism. Militarist terminology, the fetishization of uniforms, and the ceaseless praising of war and empire were all part of the effort to indoctrinate the people. An official article on fascist doctrine stated:

> [Fascism] believes neither in the possibility nor the utility of perpetual peace. . . . War alone brings up to its highest tension all human energy and puts the stamp of nobility upon the peoples who have the courage to meet it.

Mussolini, who had stated that fascism "carries the antipacifist spirit over even into the lives of individuals" and that "it is education for combat," started a series of "battles." To increase the birthrate, he started a "battle of the cradle." To encourage farmers to grow more grain, he started a "battle for wheat." To protect the national currency during the Great Depression, he started a "battle of the Lira." To increase Italian territory, he launched a "battle for land reclamation." Regardless of whether or not they were successful, these "battles" gave Mussolini outlets for his militaristic pageantry.

Total regulation of society was a constant theme of fascist propaganda, and such regulation necessarily required an effective secret police, which Mussolini had at his disposal in the form of the fascist state militia. Secret police and propaganda were the tools of fascist control and the means whereby fascism sought to realize one of Mussolini's slogans: "Nothing against the state, nothing outside the state."

Of all the institutions that had existed before the fascist takeover, only three were allowed to continue with any degree of independence: the monarchy, the army, and the church. To a large extent, these institutions were not done away with because Mussolini recognized that by using them he could obtain greater allegiance and control. A good example of this is Mussolini's reconciliation with the church.

Ever since the unification of Italy in 1870—when Rome, the last vestige of the Papal States, was brought under government control—the papacy and the Italian state had been vehemently opposed to one another. But as soon as Mussolini became prime minister in 1922, dropping his atheism and anticlericalism and replacing it with a policy of state support of the church, the church supported him. In February 1929, determined to cement his regime's relations with the church, Mussolini went to Vatican City and signed the Lateran Agreements. Under the terms of the treaty, the Italian state recognized the sovereignty of the pope within Vatican City and the papacy recognized the kingdom of Italy. The agreements also made Catholicism the state religion. church marriage and divorce laws became those of the state, and religious teaching in the schools was expanded. The church also received a substantial sum of money in the form of state bonds, which gave it a considerable financial interest in the stability of the fascist regime.

With the signing of the Lateran Agreements, Mussolini's reputation as a statesman soared. He immediately called for elections to be held in May 1929. In accordance with new fascist legislation, candidates were now proposed by the corporations. From among those nominated, the Fascist Grand Council, fascism's new ruling body, chose a list of 400 candidates that was then presented to the voters, who in turn were given the choice of voting yes or no. The pope was promised that some Catholics would be put on the list of candidates, and pastors duly instructed their congregations to vote for the list. Under this rigged system, the fascists, with the help of more physical violence and falsified election tallies, received over 98 percent of the vote. Firmly entrenched as dictator, Mussolini now gave free reign to his imperial fantasies.

Mussolini with high church officials at Vatican City. Mussolini won the Catholic church's support for fascist Italy by signing the Lateran Agreements with the Vatican in 1929. Under the pact, the Vatican and Italy recognized each other as sovereign states, ending a 60-year dispute between the two.

6

Fantasy Empire

When Mussolini became prime minister in 1922, he kept for himself two of the most important ministerial posts in the government, minister of the interior and minister of foreign affairs. As minister of the interior, Mussolini was in charge of all police responsibilities. This enabled him to control the fascist militia, whose job it was to eradicate all internal opposition. As minister of foreign affairs, Mussolini was responsible for relations between Italy and all foreign countries. In this position, he would pursue his quest to restore Italy's grandezza.

Mussolini's desire to reestablish Italian greatness had many roots. One of them was the frustration and anger that he and many Italian nationalists felt with the outcome of the Paris Peace Conference and the Treaty of St. Germain. But the most fantastic was Mussolini's idea that Italy should once again dominate the world, just as it had centuries before, during the Roman Empire. This desire motivated Mussolini in both his domestic and foreign policy.

The nation is in our hands now, and we swear to lead her back to her ways of ancient greatness.
—BENITO MUSSOLINI
after being declared prime minister of Italy

Having spent the '20s solidifying his hold as dictator at home, in the '30s Mussolini prepared to build an empire beyond Italy's borders. As the militarization of the nation intensified, Mussolini no longer wore civilian clothes during public appearances.

campo mussolini

The constant use of militaristic symbolism was meant to keep the minds of Italians focused on war, conquest, and glory. At the entrance to Campo Mussolini, near Rome, adolescent boys file past a pillar embellished with miniature tanks.

Mussolini undertook a number of measures on the domestic front. There was an enormous building campaign, and a series of archaeological excavations was begun. Old monuments were restored and new ones built. Much of this construction and restoration culminated in October 1932, which was designated Year 10 of the fascist revolution, since years were now counted from the March on Rome in October 1922. One key event of this 10th-anniversary celebration was the opening of an athletic complex named for Mussolini. The complex included an enormous stadium, massive marble statues of athletes, and a 55-foot-high marble column with the word "Duce" carved into it. That same day, Mussolini also opened a new street in Rome, the Via dell'Impero, or Road of Empire.

once again posed as the leader of an encircled, embattled country. Even some former opponents of the regime came to support the war with Ethiopia. The papacy did not utter a word of condemnation. Mussolini took full advantage of the sudden resurgence of nationalism provoked by foreign criticism of the Italian invasion, and the fascist government won the population to its cause.

On May 9, 1936, Mussolini strode out onto the balcony of the Palazzo Venezia. The speech he gave was a masterpiece of bombast and lies:

> Today, May 9, of the fourteenth year of the Fascist era, the fate of Ethiopia is sealed. All the knots were cut by our shining sword, and the African victory stands in the history of our Fatherland whole and pure as the fallen legionnaires and those who survived dreamed and wanted it. At last Italy has her empire. A Fascist empire . . . because this is the goal toward which for fourteen years the disciplined energies of the young and lusty Italians were driven. An empire at peace, because Italy wants peace for herself and for everyone and resorts to war only when compelled by the imperious, ineluctable necessities of life. A civilized empire, humanitarian toward all the peoples of Ethiopia.

Mussolini then proclaimed that the king of Italy would be known as the emperor of Ethiopia, as well.

Mussolini was intoxicated with his empire. The Italians in general, and Mussolini in particular, derived an unrealistic sense of their military strength from the episode. Now, Mussolini not only considered Italy to be the military equal of any country (which was far from true); he also failed to recognize how thoroughly corruption had infected the military and the economy.

By this time, in fact, Mussolini had very little idea of what was really happening in the country. All he ever heard were his own deluded pronouncements, and all he ever read was their repetition in the press. To win the Duce's favor and the regime's money, advisers, military men, and businessmen told Mussolini only what he wanted to hear. Thus was Mussolini a prisoner of his own fantasies.

7

Pact of Steel

The relationship between Mussolini and Adolf Hitler, leader of the National Socialist German Workers' party, or Nazi party, who became chancellor of Germany in 1933 and made himself dictator in 1934, is one of the curious aspects of international relations in the 1930s. At various times in their relationship, each followed the lead of the other. Although deceit and contempt sometimes marked their relations, there was also an element of mutual admiration.

The term fascism is generally used to describe both Italian fascism and the fascistic regime established by Hitler and the Nazis. Nazism and Italian fascism were both totalitarian and also violently anticommunist and antidemocratic. Both regimes were characterized by nationalist resentment of their respective countries' treatment at the Paris Peace Conference, and both wanted to reestablish Great Power status by means of unscrupulous diplomacy and wars of conquest. (Under the terms of the Treaty of Versailles, which was signed on June

> *Hitler, you are a genius . . . there is a bond between us dictated by destiny which was bound to become stronger and stronger.*
> —BENITO MUSSOLINI

Adolf Hitler, who modeled his own Nazi dictatorship after the fascist regime of Mussolini, declared in the early days of his political ascension: "I want precisely the same power as Mussolini exercised after the March on Rome."

Hitler's first meeting with Mussolini, in Venice in 1934. The Nazi dictator raises his arm in the fascist salute, which was based on the salute of the legionnaries of ancient Rome. D'Annunzio first revived the salute during his brief regime in Fiume, the Italian fascists copied it from him, and later the Nazis adopted it as well.

28, 1919, by the Allied powers and Germany, Germany had been stripped of a considerable amount of territory and forced to pay indemnities on a scale that eventually wrecked her economy, causing tremendous unemployment and widespread social distress. Downward revisions of the indemnities had salvaged the situation later on, but not before suffering had made the German people susceptible to Hitler's nationalistic and revenge-oriented demagoguery.)

When Hitler came to power in 1933, Mussolini had already risen to the height of his power. It is therefore understandable that throughout the 1920s and into the early 1930s, Hitler had great admiration for Mussolini and looked to Italian fascism as a model for his own regime. The Nazi salute was copied from the Italian fascists' raised-arm-and-outstretched-hand technique, and Hitler's title—Führer, or Leader—was devised in imitation of Duce. Almost from the beginning of his political career, Hitler felt that Mussolini's successful sub-version of democracy in Italy constituted solid evidence of the correctness of his own perception of politics. Influenced by Mussolini, Hitler, too, had acted with the conviction that a mass movement under strong leadership could successfully bypass the parliamentary process.

Mussolini's preeminence over Hitler was demonstrated at their first meeting in June 1934. Greeting the man who had once sent him a request for an autographed picture, Mussolini snapped to a nearby companion, "I don't like him," as Hitler got off the train.

Mussolini's first impression of Hitler did not change as a result of this meeting. Hitler failed to behave like an admiring pupil. The German dictator made it clear that he intended to influence Austrian affairs, which Mussolini considered his own preserve, and lectured Mussolini out of his book *Mein Kampf*, or *My Struggle*, a diatribe against communists and Jews. (Hitler, who was violently anti-Semitic as well as violently anticommunist, believed that the communists had caused the inflation that ruined Germany in the 1920s and that the Jews had conspired against the country for their own financial gain.)

One month after this meeting, Engelbert Dollfuss, the chancellor of Austria, was assassinated by Austrian Nazis who were attempting to stage a coup. It was common knowledge that Hitler wanted to achieve *Anschluss*, or political union, with Austria, and Mussolini, who had supported Dollfuss and had no intention of allowing a German takeover of Italy's northern neighbor, immediately announced that Italy would defend Austria against any German assault and sent 100,000 troops to the Austrian border.

For the next two years, relations between the two dictators remained distant. The situation changed in 1936. Shortly after Italy invaded Ethiopia, Hitler sent troops into the Rhineland, the area west of the Rhine River where, under the terms of the Treaty of Versailles, the Allies had forbidden Germany to station troops. He also offered to send troops to fight

General Francisco Franco, leader of Spain's nationalist forces, inspects his troops shortly before the final overthrow of the Spanish democracy in 1936. Assisted by Mussolini and Hitler, Franco became absolute dictator and head of the fascist Falange party in Spain. His rule lasted until 1975.

Galeazzo Ciano, the son of a prominent fascist, married Mussolini's daughter Edda on May 3, 1930. In 1933, Mussolini named his 30-year-old son-in-law to head the propaganda ministry; in 1936, he appointed him foreign minister.

alongside the Italians in Ethiopia, but the fighting was over before any such arrangements were made. After the conquest of Ethiopia, Hitler quickly recognized the new Italian empire. Hitler also concluded an agreement with Austria that suggested that Germany would not threaten Austria's independence. Finally, in 1936, Italy and Germany found themselves fighting side by side in Spain.

In July 1936 the fascist-nationalist commanders of Spanish army units based in Spanish Morocco rebelled against their country's democratically elected republican government, which was dominated by socialists. The rebels, who were led by General Francisco Franco, saw their revolt as a holy crusade against communism. Mussolini and Hitler, who shared Franco's antidemocratic ideals, immediately offered the rebel leader military assistance,

Hitler also demonstrated that Nazism was the equal of Italian fascism with regard to dramatic presentation. Hitler and Mussolini rode into Berlin on separate trains. During the last few miles of the journey, the engines of the two trains were aligned and traveled side by side to signify the "parallelism" of the two regimes. Mussolini's visit was a success. He came away convinced of Germany's ability to win any war. Also, the relationship between the two dictators was changing. From this time onward, Mussolini began to follow Hitler's lead.

In November 1937, Mussolini joined the Anti-Comintern Pact, an agreement originally signed by Germany and Japan to oppose communism and the Union of Soviet Socialist Republics (USSR), as Russia was now known. In December, following the earlier example of Germany, Mussolini pulled Italy out of the League of Nations.

At this time, the question of Austria's future remained a bone of contention between Italy and Germany. Hitler had never hidden his desire for Anschluss, and up until this point Mussolini had done the best he could to keep Austria independent but weak. After his visit to Germany, however, he

Mussolini, Hitler, and Victor Emmanuel III greeting crowds during the Führer's visit to Rome in 1938. Following this visit, Mussolini announced that anti-Semitic race laws would be introduced in Italy.

made it clear that the fate of Austria was now of less concern to him. He informed the German ambassador to Great Britain, Joachim von Ribbentrop, that events should be allowed to take their course but that Germany should inform Italy before making any move. Hitler, now believing that Mussolini had given him a free hand, promptly went ahead with his plan.

In February 1938, Hitler, having ordered the Austrian Nazis to stage pro-German demonstrations, pressured the Austrian chancellor, Kurt von Schuschnigg, to give the Austrian Nazi party official recognition and to appoint Nazis to top government positions. When von Schuschnigg then attempted to forestall a German takeover by declaring that a plebiscite would be held to determine whether the Austrian people favored a "free, independent, social, Christian and united Austria," the Germans sent an ultimatum demanding his resignation. Von Schuschnigg then resigned in favor of leading Austrian Nazi Arthur Seyss-Inquart, who invited the German army to occupy Austria. Without consulting Mussolini and giving him just a few hours' notice, Germany invaded on March 12, 1938, and Anschluss was proclaimed the following day. When Hitler's messenger informed Mussolini of what had taken place, Mussolini announced that he was pleased. When Hitler, who had been afraid that Mussolini's response might be extremely unfavorable and even military in nature, was informed of Mussolini's response, he remarked, "I will never forget, whatever may happen. If he should ever need any help or be in danger, he can be convinced that I shall stick by him, whatever may happen, even if the whole world were against him."

Hitler's failure to inform Mussolini of his intentions was the beginning of a pattern. Mussolini recognized that he was becoming the junior partner in the relationship. The more Mussolini bowed to Hitler, the more Italy bowed before the power of Nazi Germany. Mussolini's support at home actually suffered as a result of his having given in to the Führer. The Anschluss did not warm Italian hearts to Hitler.

In August 1938, Mussolini proposed a set of racial laws based on those already in effect in Germany. Thinking in terms of race was not new to Mussolini. Before and during the Ethiopian war, he made public statements in which he said Africans were racially inferior to Italians. In his "battle of the cradle," he spoke of preserving the racial purity of Italy. His remark to Ciano that he wanted to reforest the Apennine Mountains in order to make the climate more severe so that the weaklings would be killed off and the Italian "race" would become more hearty was another example of his racism.

But after Hitler's visit in 1938, a new kind of racist thinking emerged in Italy: anti-Semitism. Jews made up only one-tenth of one percent of the Italian population, and there were a number of Jews in the Fascist party, some holding prominent positions. During the early 1930s, Mussolini had scoffed at Hitler's anti-Semitism. Italy had given refuge to Jews who had fled from Nazi Germany. Now, however, the Italian propaganda machine went to work

A Czechoslovakian woman weeps as she salutes German troops marching through the city of Eger in October 1938. As a result of the Munich conference, Germany had annexed part of Czechoslovakia. As mediator at Munich, Mussolini secretly helped Hitler achieve the annexation.

A 1934 election billboard featuring the Duce's face surrounded by the word *si* ("yes") adorns the façade of the Fascist party headquarters in Rome. Mussolini's image was displayed everywhere, accompanied by reminders of his infallibility and exhortations to fight for fascism.

to cultivate racism. Newspapers printed an absurd statement by a number of professors that Italians were actually Aryans of unmixed stock. Racist laws and terminology were taken from Germany. Italian racist laws were not as harsh as those of Germany, but they caused great suffering nonetheless. Jewish teachers and students were kicked out of public schools, and some Jews lost their jobs. Families were broken up, and many left the country. Later, during World War II, more than 8,000 Italian Jews— almost 15 percent of the country's Jewish population—were sent to concentration camps.

Having annexed Austria in March 1938, Hitler next decided to press yet another territorial claim. The object of his attentions was the predominantly German-speaking Sudetenland region of Czechoslovakia, an independent democratic republic bordering on southeastern Germany. At this point British prime minister Neville Chamberlain resorted to appeasement, a method of conducting foreign policy whereby one makes concessions to an enemy if doing so is the only alternative to war. In September 1938, Chamberlain and French prime minister Edouard Daladier traveled to Munich, Germany, for a conference with Hitler and Mussolini. The British had asked Mussolini to intervene in the dispute as a mediator, and Mussolini had accepted. At the meeting, Mussolini submitted a proposal for resolving the conflict that he and Hitler had already secretly agreed upon. The leaders of the two most powerful democracies in Europe accepted the proposal and announced that they would support Hitler's claim to the Sudetenland if he would agree not to invade Czechoslovakia. Under the terms of the agreements reached at the conference (at which no Czechoslovakian representatives were present), Czechoslovakia was forced to cede 10,000 square miles of its territory to Germany, 5,000 to Hungary, and a smaller area to Poland.

Mussolini's role in the negotiations had been minimal, but he used the occasion to parade as a great statesman. He returned to Rome a hero, the savior of the peace. He basked in all the praise and acclamation the Italians gave him, but he felt a burning contempt for the Italians for desiring peace instead of war.

Shortly after the Munich conference, German propaganda encouraged disaffection among Czechoslovakia's minorities, forcing the Czechoslovakian government to grant self-rule to the country's Slovak and Carpatho-Ukrainian populations. Then, on March 12, 1939, Germany's state-controlled newspapers carried false reports that Czechoslovakia's German minority was also being persecuted. On March 13 the German foreign ministry summoned Josef Tiso, a Slovak politican and

Mussolini invaded Albania, a small country on the Adriatic coast of the Balkan peninsula, in April 1939, five months before the start of World War II. The Albanians offered virtually no resistance, but the disorganized and ill-equipped Italian forces still had much difficulty occupying the country.

churchman, to Berlin and ordered him to proclaim Slovak independence. On March 15, Emil Hacha, the president of Czechoslovakia, was informed by Hitler that German troops had already crossed his country's borders and that a full-scale invasion would be launched unless he signed an agreement making the Czech provinces of Bohemia and Moravia German protectorates. Hacha had no choice but to sign the agreement. Czechoslovakia had been wiped off the map of Europe. Great Britain and France did nothing.

Mussolini, once again, had not been informed of Hitler's intentions. Praised by his people for the Munich agreements that Hitler had just repudiated, Mussolini became increasingly concerned about his image. "The Italians would laugh at me; every time Hitler occupies a country he sends me a message," he said privately. Mussolini then tried to turn the situation to his advantage. If Hitler could invade Czechoslovakia with little protest, why should not Italy invade Albania?

It is not terribly clear what Italy had to gain from invading and occupying Albania other than provid-

8

"Appointment with History"

Mussolini and Hitler undoubtedly had many things in common, but there were also considerable differences between the two men and the regimes they established. Mussolini, regardless of all his heroic talk, could not match Hitler's ruthless determination and ability to launch an aggressive war to dominate Europe. However, spurred on by Hitler's successful aggression, Mussolini increasingly fell victim to ever more fantastic delusions of grandeur. The differences between the two dictators can nowhere be seen more clearly than in their countries' preparation for, and conduct during, World War II.

Although in May 1939 the Germans had agreed with the Italians that there should be three more years of peace, Hitler had already decided to attack Poland "at the first suitable opportunity." In June, Mussolini boasted to Hitler that if the Germans wanted to attack right away, Italy would be ready.

> *Victory will soon place Italy at the very top rank of nations where she will be able to direct the whole life of Europe . . . the bigger the war becomes, the greater the reward of booty and reparations.*
> —BENITO MUSSOLINI

Mussolini came out of a long family tradition of aggressiveness and violence, but with a flare for dictatorial camp that was truly his own he, along with Adolf Hitler, gave barbarism a modern face. With impassioned public speeches he indulged his delirious fantasies of grandeur and intimidated an entire nation.

Some of the 70,000 female soldiers who paraded before Mussolini to celebrate the 20th anniversary of fascism in 1939. Despite such ostensible displays of power, the Italian military was actually weak, hobbled by a badly disorganized command structure and antiquated weaponry.

A few days later, when it became clear that Hitler took this boast seriously, Mussolini sent Ciano to Germany to desperately ask Hitler to wait another three or more years before starting the war. The Germans not only ignored Ciano's pleas, they issued a communiqué saying that Italy fully supported the German position. Thus, Mussolini and Ciano learned once and for all that Hitler regarded Italy as a junior partner in the Axis.

Many Italians and some fascists were not in favor of fighting on Hitler's side. Some fascists even called for Mussolini to renounce the Pact of Steel. Mussolini proved indecisive, repeatedly changing his mind.

Even more important was the question of whether or not Italy was prepared to fight a war. In his less hysterical moments, Mussolini knew that Italy was not ready in the least. This had already been made clear by the invasion of Albania.

Workmen pile sandbags in front of public buildings in Milan in July 1940, one month after Italy entered the war. Mussolini said several times in private that he hoped the Allies would bomb Italian cities to "toughen up" the Italian people.

The political and economic features that had become the norm in Italy had undermined the country's military capability. Corruption had become a way of life. The fascist state had become one big machine to pass out money and titles to the rich and powerful. Just as in the corporations, so it was in the military that fascists were given positions for which they had no qualifications. Bribes, false contracts, and payoffs were all-pervasive. Businesses were run in the same way. For example, the boots that were supplied to the Italian military were often found to have soles made of cardboard.

The condition of the military was unbelievable. In 1939, at the outbreak of World War II, most Italian artillery dated from 1918. The rifles issued to the soldiers dated from 1891. There was a serious shortage of ammunition. Of the air force's 3,000 planes,

German field marshal Erwin Rommel (center), nicknamed "the Desert Fox," commanded the Afrika Korps and oversaw the Axis war effort in North Africa after Italian offensives were disastrously botched by Mussolini early in 1941. By 1943, all of Italy's African colonies — Libya, Ethiopia, and Somaliland — were lost.

only 1,000 were in any condition to fly. Mussolini boasted about his 70 divisions, but in fact there were only 10 fully effective frontline divisions. The country had only two searchlights. The clothing of the troops was inadequate for the conditions, and there were not enough uniforms. Reconnaissance aircraft were lacking, and pilots were poorly trained. There were no plans for night fighting, there were no arrangements for cooperation between the navy and the air force, and though the navy was in relatively good shape, it was short of fuel.

That Mussolini could even consider fighting a war under these circumstances, over the objections of several leading generals, is proof of how little grasp he had on reality and of his willingness to put the Italians through great hardship in pursuit of his own glory. In 1943, Mussolini himself admitted to one of his admirals that Italy had been much better prepared for war in 1915 than in 1939.

By the end of August 1939, Mussolini was finally persuaded to face the fact that Italy was in no position to go to war immediately. He had to recognize that Hitler was once again going ahead with his aggressive plans despite what the Duce thought and regardless of what assistance he might offer. Mussolini had to recognize that despite 17 years of raving on and on about war and its glory and after raising a new generation in his militaristic organizations, the Italian "race" had not become any more warlike. Most devastating for his ego was that he could not deliver on all his boasting. He told Hitler that Italy was not ready for war and that the Italians would not fight.

Mussolini explained his decision to Hitler by alluding to the additional time that Italy needed to prepare. In a clever ploy, he also informed Hitler that if Germany could supply him with 17 million tons of vital supplies, Italy could join him. Hitler, who was planning to invade Poland in a matter of days, could not part with so much war matériel. When Germany invaded Poland on September 1, 1939, Italy adopted an attitude that she called "non-belligerency." On September 3, France and Great Britain, which were pledged to assist the Poles, declared war on Germany.

For the remainder of 1939, Mussolini, like many of his countrymen, had strong anti-German feelings. He was both admiring and jealous of Germany's military prowess and Hitler's glory. Throughout this time, Hitler courted Mussolini. He did not scold him for not living up to the Pact of Steel but sought to pull Italy into the war. Hitler's quick victories, Mussolini's incorrect assumption that the war would be short, and his concern that Italy had to enter the war without delay to get its share of the spoils of victory all convinced Mussolini that Italy had to go to war, prepared or not.

On June 10, 1940, by which time the German army had crushed the French and forced the British to withdraw their forces from Europe, Mussolini, without consulting his cabinet or the Fascist Grand Council, declared war on France and Great Britain. To keep his "appointment with history," Mussolini had to act quickly. France had already asked for an armistice. Mussolini instructed his generals that the army only had to prepare for a defensive war. All he was looking for, he said, were a few thousand dead so he could attend the peace conference as a victor.

Although he was informed that the army needed 20 days to switch to an offensive stance, Mussolini ordered an attack in three days. Unprepared and improvising, the Italians marched on southeastern France. Although France was already all but beaten, the Italian army made a miserable showing. On June 22, 1940, the French signed an armistice with Germany, the real conqueror. Three days later the French surrendered to the Italians as well. But while Germany was crushing French forces to the north, all the Italian forces could manage was the taking of just 13 villages while losing over 600 dead to France's 37.

The Italian army's performance in France was sobering to the generals but not to Mussolini, who was unwilling to acknowledge the unpreparedness of the military. This, coupled with his incompetent command, was a sure prescription for disaster.

World War II was the "supreme game," the climax of fascism. For almost 20 years, Mussolini had hectored the Italian people with the promise of total war, a "titanic enterprise" that would make Italians the masters of Europe.

A Russian family near the ruins of their home, destroyed during Hitler's 1941 invasion of the USSR. Mussolini sent thousands of Italian soldiers to the Russian front to share in what he thought would be an easy German victory. But by 1943, the invasion forces were routed, having suffered overwhelming losses.

Much of his behavior was simply incomprehensible. For example, he would often fail to inform his generals of changes in strategy and tactics, leaving them to learn of their armies' invasions by hearing it over the radio. Furthermore, he was still mistakenly convinced that the war would not last through the winter. Consequently, and again without consulting his chiefs of staff, he demobilized 300,000 men so they could assist with the harvest at home. Despite this, he did not give up his plans for further aggression.

> *The liquidation of Greece will be profitable and easy.*
>
> —BENITO MUSSOLINI

In a move intended to secure gains for Italy at little cost, the Italian army occupied British Somaliland in August 1940. The Italians did not move on Suez, which would have been far more important strategically. In September, Mussolini pushed his generals to move against Egypt, which was then a British protectorate. This attack brought an early and limited victory, but the Italian military was incapable of following up on this initial thrust. Foolishly, Mussolini failed to concentrate his forces on this effort; even more foolishly, he refused to accept when Hitler offered assistance.

In December 1940 the British launched a counteroffensive. The Italians were thrown back all the way to Libya, and 100,000 of them were taken prisoner. Faced with a potential Axis disaster, Hitler had to bail out the Duce. German general Erwin Rommel assumed command of the Führer's Afrika Korps and took charge of the Axis operation in North Africa. Rommel won a succession of stunning victories over the British. But the problem for Mussolini was that Rommel did not move into East Africa, where Italy's empire lay. By the end of February 1941, Somalia had fallen to the British, and Haile Selassie had returned to Ethiopia, which had been liberated by a joint British, Ethiopian, and South African force. The Italian empire in Africa had ceased to exist.

North Africa was not the only scene of Mussolini's disastrous folly. Back in October 1940, Mussolini decided to strike at Greece, an invasion planned against the background of the major demobilization he had ordered. His generals informed him that any move against Greece should be put off until the spring. Mussolini would brook no delay. He gave his generals less than two weeks to prepare. The invasion took place on October 28, without the knowledge of his army chief of staff. The date was chosen not for any logistical reason, but to coincide with the anniversary of the March on Rome.

Within a few days, the poorly equipped Italian troops were in full retreat. Mussolini's absurd scheme to invade Greece and let Hitler learn of his victory "from the newspapers" turned into a sheepish request for German assistance to avoid a total rout. With the arrival of German troops and bombers to vanquish Greece and neighboring Yugoslavia and thus save Italy from humiliation, the tenor of the war changed decisively for the Italians. Increasingly, Germany came to dominate Italy's military and society. It was becoming clear that soon there would be a large German military presence in Italy itself.

Mussolini's admiration and resentment of the Führer grew daily. Hitler continued to be courteous and friendly to Mussolini in their many meetings and in their correspondence. Rather than accept the Italian contribution on the battlefield, Hitler preferred to see Italians work in his factories, where hundreds of thousands of Italians labored during the war. Often their treatment was not much better than that of the conquered populations working in the same factories. Such activity was not suited to Mussolini's grandiose image of himself and Italy. Nor was it suited to strengthening the bond between Italians and Germans. As German control over Italian affairs grew, so too did anti-German sentiment among the Italians.

At the end of November 1941, the Japanese informed Mussolini that they were about to launch a preemptive attack against the Americans, who had not yet entered the war. Mussolini gave the plan his full support. On December 7 the Japanese attacked the American naval base at Pearl Harbor in Hawaii. The United States now joined the war against Japan, Germany, and Italy. Mussolini, contemptuous of the Americans and what he considered their decadence and weakness, expressed his delight.

But the Italians' discontent with the war grew. Rather than the promised "lightning victory," the war was dragging on, bringing them repeated defeats and unmasking Mussolini and fascism as hollow and destructive. In early 1942, there were strikes throughout Italy. Antifascist sentiment was on the rise. Clandestine newspapers began to appear. Inflation and a growing black market resulted from shortages. The more apparent these developments, the tighter the Nazi stranglehold on the country became.

Clara Petacci, Mussolini's mistress for 10 years. By 1942, with the war going badly and Mussolini showing more pronounced signs of personal instability, their relationship became public knowledge and the subject of widespread gossip. Mussolini's already faltering prestige was further hurt as a result.

Mussolini, however, was not the only dictator to make gross miscalculations. In June 1941, Hitler's armies invaded the USSR. Although there were early stunning victories, this course of action would be the undoing of Nazi Germany. Forever grasping for glory, Mussolini insisted on sending 200,000 soldiers to the German-Soviet front. By early 1943, 50 percent of those troops were dead or wounded.

By the end of 1942, there was little cause for Axis optimism. Soviet forces were poised to crush the German Sixth Army at Stalingrad and turn the tide of war in the east, and U.S. and British forces had landed in North Africa.

Throughout this time, Mussolini's physical and mental condition continued to decline. His ulcers caused him considerable pain, and he was more irritable. People took it as a sign of his growing eccentricity and lack of control that he installed one of his mistresses, Clara Petacci, in an apartment at his palace.

In his meetings with Hitler, Mussolini was now totally subservient. His dislike for the Germans continued to grow, and he even complained about Hitler. But much of his contempt was reserved for the Italians. They were, he said, a race of sheep. He delighted in the bombing of Italian cities and the severe conditions the population endured. All this, he said, would strengthen the race.

As the fate of Italian forces continued to worsen in 1943, Mussolini's delusions came to play an ever greater role. He hinted at the existence of a "secret weapon" that simply did not exist. In June he told the Italians that the enemy was incapable of making any further advances. The very next month, Allied forces were in Sicily, on Italian soil. On July 19, Rome was bombed for the first time in the war.

A number of fascists now began to consider removing Mussolini. Military leaders, some of the old liberal politicians, and the king had similar thoughts. The decisive move was finally made by the Fascist Grand Council on the night of July 24, 1943. This was the council's first meeting in three and a half years. Fearful of Mussolini's reaction and uncertain of the outcome of the steps they were tak-

9

Mussolini's Last Days

Mussolini's fall from power did not precipitate any fascist uprising or even public protests. The only demonstrations were those of Italian citizens who destroyed fascist symbols and pulled down statues of Mussolini.

The new government was headed by Marshal Pietro Badoglio, the chief of general staff from 1925 to 1940. In 1922, Badoglio was one of the generals who advised Victor Emmanuel III that all the army needed to stop the March on Rome and quash the fascist bid for power was the order to do so. Later that decade, after Mussolini had taken over, Badoglio countered a persistent guerrilla war against Italian rule in Libya with executions, civilian internment camps, and poison gas — tactics he would later use again in the Ethiopian war. Throughout the 1930s, he assured Mussolini that the Italian military was strong and able to win a world war. In autumn 1940, when Greece successfully repulsed an Italian invasion to which Badoglio had been opposed, he angrily pointed out to Mussolini that the Greek campaign was a disaster for which the Duce was to blame. Badoglio was fired. Less than two years later, he was chosen by the king to take over the premiership from Mussolini.

> If I'd been successful, not one person in Italy would have questioned the morality of my entering the war on Hitler's side. In politics there is no morality — only success or failure.
> —BENITO MUSSOLINI

Italians reacted to Mussolini's ouster by pulling down statues of the Duce and defacing fascist symbols. In Allied-controlled Messina, Sicily, a portrait of Mussolini was used for target practice. Even Fascist party members in Axis-controlled portions of Italy greeted the Duce's fall from power with relief.

LA STORICA SEDUTA NELLA QUALE IL DUCE SOTTOPONE AL GRAN CONSIGLIO
L'USCITA IMMEDIATA DELL'ITALIA DALLA SOCIETÀ DELLE NAZIONI.

LVCE

After his imprisonment, the Germans rescued Mussolini and installed him as head of a puppet regime in northern Italy. He then staged a trial of the Fascist Grand Council members who had ousted him. Five were executed, including Marinelli (3rd from left), Ciano (8th from left), and De Bono (11th from left).

Badoglio immediately sent out peace feelers to the Allies in an effort to extricate Italy from its increasingly hopeless position in the war. On September 8, an armistice was signed, but the Germans immediately took over all of Italy north of Naples.

For six weeks following Mussolini's arrest on July 25, the new government moved the former Duce from one hiding place to another. But these efforts were in vain. On September 12, 1943, four days after the Italian armies surrendered to the Allies, Mussolini was "rescued" by German paratroopers in a daring raid on the mountain lodge where he was then being held. The Italian soldiers guarding him put up no resistance.

The German rescue was the first step in a scheme to prop up Mussolini in power. Yet Hitler no longer had any sentimentality about the role Mussolini was to play. Mussolini was to be a mere figurehead. His role was to try to show that fascism had not collapsed and to try to prevent any more Italians from going over to the antifascist cause.

Mussolini's new regime was called the Republic of Salò. It took its name from a small town on Lake Garda in northern Italy, where its offices were located, well within the German-controlled half of the country. Mussolini's new party was known as the Fascist Republican party. Neither the new party nor the new regime had an independent existence; they were creations of the Germans, set up for the benefit of the Nazi war effort. Every move made by Mussolini and his regime was overseen by the Germans.

The only action that could have conferred upon the new fascist regime any semblance of independence from Germany would have been to raise an army and thereby contribute to the Axis military cause. But Hitler was determined to prevent this. He did not trust the Italians, particularly after Badoglio's government in the south had declared war against Germany in October. Italy as a country was not to be defended; it was merely to be an arena of battle for the Germans against the Allies and the partisans, the underground antifascist forces.

Edda Mussolini bestows the fascist salute upon her father during a rally in 1927. In 1943, despite Edda's desperate pleas, Mussolini had her husband Ciano put to death. She was not allowed to visit Ciano in the days before his execution.

Mussolini's fascism had not just brought Italy to ruin, fascism itself had disintegrated. In the Republic of Saló, Mussolini's philosophy—always an incoherent jumble of ideas united by one overriding principle, the seizure and exercise of absolute power — changed once more. Up until 1922, Mussolini had been a staunch republican, opposed to kings and monarchy. When he realized that the monarchy could strengthen his regime, he put his republicanism aside. But now, because the king had had a hand in removing him from power in July 1943, he reverted to republicanism. The regime at Saló was called a republic, and Mussolini once again gave vent to his antimonarchism.

Mussolini had started his political career as a socialist. But when it became clear around 1920 that virulent antisocialism would provide him with the means to gain power, he quickly jumped from the extreme left to the extreme right, where he stayed until he was ousted as Duce. Now, at Saló, he blamed the capitalists and the middle class for his

Italian partisans fought against the German forces occupying the northern half of Italy while the Allies tried to move up from the south. Fighting was fierce and progress was slow. Rome fell to the Allies in June 1944, and by spring 1945 the final offensive to take northern Italy was finally under way.

Finally, on April 27, Mussolini joined a German transport column trying to escape Italy through the mountains into Austria. A partisan roadblock stopped the column and agreed to let the Germans pass but demanded to inspect the unit for any Italians. Mussolini was discovered wearing the coat and helmet of a German soldier and taken prisoner.

In the afternoon of April 28, 1945, Benito Mussolini and Clara Petacci were executed by partisans. The next day, their bodies were taken to Milan and hung upside down in a public square. Less than two weeks later, Hitler had committed suicide, Germany was defeated, and the war in Europe came to an end. Italy was finally free of fascism and the Duce.

After keeping Mussolini's coffin concealed in a monastery for 12 years, the Italian government returned it to his widow Rachele in 1957. The body of Benito Mussolini was buried alongside those of his parents in the family vault near Predappio, his birthplace.

Further Reading

DeGrand, Alexander. *Italian Fascism: Its Origins and Development.* Lincoln and London: University of Nebraska Press, 1982.

Fermi, Laura, *Mussolini.* Chicago: University of Chicago Press, 1961.

Kirkpatrick, Ivone. *Mussolini: A Study in Power.* New York: Hawthorn Books, 1964.

Salvemini, Gaetano. *Under the Axe of Fascism.* New York: Viking, 1936.

Smith, Denis Mack. *Mussolini: A Biography.* New York: Random House, 1982.

———. *Mussolini's Roman Empire.* New York: Penguin, 1976.

Wiskemann, Elizabeth. *Fascism in Italy: Its Development and Influence.* New York: St. Martin's, 1970.

Chronology

July 29, 1883	Benito Mussolini is born near Predappio, Italy
July 1901	Graduates from school with a diploma in teaching
July 1902	Goes to Switzerland; becomes socialist agitator
Nov. 1904	Returns to Italy and enters army
1909	Becomes secretary of Trent (Austria) Chamber of Labor
Sept. 1909	Expelled from Austria
1910	Appointed secretary of Forlì Socialist party
Sept. 1911	Begins five-month jail term for fomenting violent opposition to Libyan war
July 1912	Gives speech to expel reformists at Socialist Party Congress; elected to party's executive committee
Dec. 1, 1912	Appointed editor of Socialist party newspaper *Avanti!*
Oct. 20, 1914	Forced to resign editorship of *Avanti!* for supporting Italian intervention in World War I
Nov. 1914	Starts publication of interventionist newspaper *Il Popolo D'Italia*; is expelled from Socialist party
May 24, 1915	Italy enters World War I
Feb. 23, 1917	Mussolini wounded in army training exercise
Nov. 11, 1918	World War I ends
March 23, 1919	Mussolini founds Fascist party
1920	Workers occupy factories; conservatives sponsor Fascist antisocialist squads
Sept. 1919–Dec. 1920	D'Annunzio's occupation of Fiume
Oct. 28–30, 1922	"March on Rome"; Mussolini becomes prime minister
1925	Consolidation of dictatorship
June 1934	First meeting between Mussolini and Hitler
Oct. 2, 1935	Italy invades Ethiopia
April 7,1939	Italy invades Albania
May 1939	Italian-German Pact of Steel
Sept. 1, 1939	Germany invades Poland; World War II begins
June 10, 1940	Italy enters war, invading France
July 1943	Allied forces land in Sicily, bomb Rome
July 25, 1943	Mussolini stripped of power and arrested
Sept. 23, 1943	Rescued by Germans and installed as head of Republic of Salò
June 1944	Rome falls to Allies
April 28, 1945	Mussolini executed by partisans

Index

Addis Ababa, 72
Afrika Corps, 96
Albania, 86–87, 90
Anschluss, 77, 81–82
Anti-Comintern Pact, 81
Arditi, 50–51
Austria, 77, 81–82, 85, 107
Austria-Hungary, 40, 44, 47
Avanti!, 29, 38, 40–41, 43–44, 51
Badoglio, Pietro, 101–3, 106
Bakunin, Mikhail, 25
Balabanoff, Angelica, 35, 38, 43
Balbo, Italo, 16
Berlin, 79, 81, 86
Bianchi, Michele, 16, 19
Bissolati, Leonida, 38
Blackshirts, 15, 19, 56–57
Bohemia, 86
Bonomi, Ivanoe, 38, 106
Bosnia, 40
Bourgeoisie, 26
British Somaliland, 96
Bulge, Battle of the, 106
Chamberlain, Neville, 85
Ciano, Galeazzo, 79, 83, 87, 90, 105
Comintern, 48
Corfu, 57
Corporatism, 61
Czechoslovakia, 85–86
Daladier, Edouard, 85
D'Annunzio, Gabriele, 45, 47, 51–52
De Bono, Emilio, 16, 105
De Vecchi, Cesare Maria, 16
Dollfuss, Engelbert, 77
Dopolavero, 62
Eden, Anthony, 71
Egypt, 96
Engels, Friedrich, 26
Eritrea, 37, 70
Ethiopia, 70–73, 77–78, 96, 101
Facta, Luigi, 17
Fascio Italiano di Combattimento, 49
Fascist Grand Council, 65, 93, 98, 105
Fascist Republican party, 103
First Congress of the Third (Communist) International. *See* Comintern
First International, 26
Fiume, 51–52, 57
Forlimpopoli, 28

Forli province, 23, 37–38
Forward!. See Avanti!
France, 38, 40, 44, 47, 86, 93–94
Franco, Francisco, 78–79
Franz Ferdinand, archduke, 40
Futurists, 51
German Social Democratic party, 41
Germany, 40, 44, 46, 75–87, 89–90, 93–94, 96–98, 107
Giolitti, Giovanni, 37, 43, 53, 106
Gorizia, 36
Gradisca, 36
Grandi, Dino, 99
Great Britain, 38, 40, 44, 47, 86, 93
Greece, 96–97, 101
Gualtieri, 31
Guidi, Rachele (wife), 45, 63
Hacha, Emil, 86
Haile Selassie, emperor of Ethiopia, 71, 96
Hitler, Adolf, 75–83, 85–87, 89, 93, 96, 98, 102–3, 107
Hungary, 85
Internazionalisti, 31
Isonzo River, 45
Istria, 36, 45, 47
Italia irredenta, 36, 45, 51
Italian Combat Band. *See Fascio Italiano di Combattimento*
Italian Socialist party, 29, 32–33, 38, 40, 44, 50–51, 56–57, 106
Japan, 81, 97
Juarez, Benito, 26
Julius Caesar, 62, 69
Lateran Agreements, 65
Lausanne, 33
League of Nations, 47, 71–72, 81
Lenin, Vladimir Ilich, 46, 48
Libya, 37–38, 43, 96, 101
Maltoni, Rosa (mother), 24, 26–27
Manganelli, 14
March on Rome, 15–16, 18, 21, 53, 55, 68, 96, 101
Marinetti, Filippo, 51
Marx, Karl, 25–26, 46
Massawa, 70
Massimalisti, 33
Matteotti, Giacomo, 57–58, 60
Maximum program, 32, 38
Mein Kampf (Hitler), 77

Milan,   16, 18, 20–21, 40, 49, 51, 106–7
Minimum program,   32
Moravia,   86
Munich,   85
Mussolini, Alessandro (father),   25–27
Mussolini, Arnaldo (brother),   26
Mussolini, Benito,
    anticlericalism of,   34–35
    birth of fascism and,   49–51
    breaks with socialists,   44
    career as socialist,   26–29, 31–38,
       40–41
    death,   107
    deposed,   99
    early years,   23–28
    establishes dictatorship,   59–60
    family and romantic life,   63
    foreign policy of,   67, 69–73, 77–82,
       85–87, 89–90, 93–98
    ill health of,   98
    institutionalizes racism,   83–84
    as journalist,   36–38, 40–41, 43–44
    marriage,   45
    military service in World War I,   45
    relationship with Hitler,   75–83, 85–87,
       89–90, 93, 96–98, 102, 106
    rise of fascist movement,   13–15
    runs for parliament,   40
    used as puppet by Germans,   102–6
    works as schoolteacher,   31, 33, 36
Mussolini, Edda (daughter),   45, 105
Mussolini, Edvidge (sister),   27
Mussolini, Vittorio (son),   45
My Life as a Rebel (Balabanoff),   35
National Committee for Liberation,   106
National Socialist German Workers' party,
    75
Nazi. *See* National Socialist German Workers'
    party
Oneglia,   36
Ottoman Empire,   37–38, 47
Pact of Steel,   87, 90, 93
Papal States,   65
Paris Peace Conference,   46–47, 49, 51, 67,
    75
People of Italy, The. See Popolo d'Italia, Il
Perugia,   16
Petacci, Clara,   63, 98, 106–107
Poland,   85, 89, 93

Popolo d'Italia, Il,   19–20, 44–45
Predappio,   23, 28, 31
Proletariat,   25
PSI. *See* Italian Socialist party
Quadrumviri,   16, 20, 105
Quirinale,   17, 21
Reggio Emilia,   38
Republic of Salo,   102–5
Rhineland,   77
Ribbentrop, Joachim von,   82
Romagna, the,   23–25, 28, 34
Roman Catholic church,   23, 57, 64–65
Rome,   13, 15, 18, 20, 47, 60, 65, 68, 79, 98
Rommel, Erwin,   96
Rossi, Cesare,   58
Royal Normal School,   28
Russia,   40, 44, 46. *See also* Union of Soviet
    Socialist Republics
St. Germain, Treaty of,   47, 67
Salandra, Antonio,   44
Sarajevo,   40
Schuschnigg, Kurt von,   82
Second International of Social Democratic
    Parties,   26, 40–41, 48
Serbia,   40
Seyss-Inquart, Arthur,   82
Sicily,   98
Smith, Denis Mack,   72
Somalia,   37, 70, 96
South Tyrol,   36, 47
Spanish civil war,   78–79
Spanish Morocco,   78–79
Squadri,   14
Squadristi. See Blackshirts
Stalingrad,   98
State capitalism. *See* Corporatism
Sudetenland,   85
Suez Canal,   71, 96
Tiso, Josef,   85
Treaty of Versailles,   75–77
Trent,   36
Trentino,   36–37, 45, 47
Trieste,   36, 45
Union of Soviet Socialist Republics,   81. *See*
    also Russia
United States,   47
Verdi, Giussepe,   29
Victor Emmanuel III, king of Italy,   16–18,
    20–21, 36, 59, 98–99, 101, 106

Wal Wal, 71
Wilson, Woodrow, 47
World War I, 40–41, 43–45

World War II, 93
Yugoslavia, 40, 51, 57,
  97

Larry Hartenian received his Ph.D. from Rutgers University, where he specialized in modern and 20th-century European history. He has taught at several universities, including Rutgers, the University of Cincinnati, and the University of New Hampshire.

Arthur M. Schlesinger, jr., taught history at Harvard for many years and is currently Albert Schweitzer Professor of the Humanities at City University of New York. He is the author of numerous highly praised works in American history and has twice been awarded the Pulitzer Prize. He served in the White House as special assistant to Presidents Kennedy and Johnson.

PICTURE CREDITS